Administration and Management

Administration and Management

A Selected and Annotated Bibliography

by

William G. Hills
André W. Van Rest
Richard C. Kearney
Stephen T. Smith

UNIVERSITY OF OKLAHOMA PRESS : NORMAN

By William G. Hills

Conducting the People's Business: The Framework and Functions of Public Administration (editor, with others; Norman, 1973)
Administration and Management: A Selected and Annotated Bibliography (with others; Norman, 1975)

Library of Congress Cataloging in Publication Data
Main entry under title:

Administration and management.

  Includes indexes.
  1. Management—Bilbiography. 2. Organization—Bibliography.
I. Hills, William G., 1937–
Z7164.07A35   016.6584   75–4963
ISBN 0-8061-1284-0
ISBN 0-8061-1285-9 pbk.

Copyright 1975 by the University of Oklahoma Press, Publishing Division of the University. Composed and printed at Norman, Oklahoma, U.S.A., by the University of Oklahoma Press. First edition.

PREFACE

THE PURPOSE of this selected and annotated bibliography is to aid administrators in the formal study of administration and to help those who wish to update or supplement their knowledge in specific areas.

It was written for *public* administrators, especially those in human-service organizations, but it should be valuable to business managers in the private sector who recognize the interdependence of business and its political, social, and cultural environment.

Works on administration are invariably prepared for a university audience, and their usefulness to the practicing administrator is often of secondary concern. As a result, administrators wishing to learn more about their craft often must wrestle with information that is less than relevant to their needs.

Today an abundance of printed material overloads communication channels and threatens to inundate people in organizations. The result is that useful information is often thrown out with the extraneous material.

Implicit in the authors' work is the belief that there is a connection between good management and the utilization of knowledge and that utilization improves with selectivity; hence this *selected* bibliography of those works we believe to be most relevant to the administrator's task. The primary criteria used to select a book for inclusion were that: (1) it should be useful to public human-service administrators; (2) practical works should take precedence over theoretical works; (3) no single author need appear more than twice; (4) books of readings should be kept to a minimum; and (5) books listed should be in print or available at the public library.

We believe that the degree of administrative competence in government determines the viability of our democratic society. Our history, and especially its recent record, demonstrates the great value of a well-trained, responsive, and responsible civil service. But the civil service cannot function at its best when private organizations ignore or fail to grasp the importance of performing responsibly in an open, democratic system. In this regard it is perhaps time to urge business to operate a little more like government rather than to argue that government ought to operate more like business.

For those in business administration this bibliography can provide a fresh perspective; for those in public administration it should provide valuable assistance in their work.

The bibliography consists of six parts. Part I covers the "Development, Scope, and Emphasis" of administration. Books dealing with "The Organization"—theory, behavior, and development—are listed in Part II. Part III, "The Administrative Process," includes works on decision making, planning and budgeting, leadership and motivation, communications and control, and evaluation. Part IV, "Personnel," is devoted to personnel management, manpower, and collective bargaining. Part V, "The Administrative Environment," lists books dealing with public and clientele relations; the formulation, passage, and execution of public policy; intergovernmental relations; and the role of values and technology in administration. The works listed in Part VI, "Comparative Administration," though largely theoretical, will aid those functioning in administrative positions abroad and those connected in any way with foreign bureaucracies, public or private. It is our conviction that a different approach can sometimes serve as a catalyst for new thinking.

The two appendices provide a selection of widely read journals and a list of handbooks and general reference works. Indexes of authors and work titles are provided to help the reader focus on particular writers and works.

Acknowledgments

THE IDEA for this annotated bibliography grew out of an earlier publication: Jagdish T. Danak and William H. Keown, *Administration and Management: A Selected and Annotated Bibliography* (Monograph Series No. 1, Regional Rehabilitation Research Institute. University of Oklahoma, April, 1969). The monograph was well received and was in demand internationally. It went out of print in 1971. This new bibliography, containing over two hundred entries, is oriented more toward the public administrator than the earlier work and is more comprehensive, in terms of the administrative areas covered. We have retained, in modified form, approximately twenty of the annotations from the monograph, primarily classics, and for those we are indebted to its authors.

This bibliography is the result of the efforts of several persons. William G. Hills recognized the need for a bibliography in administration and management that included works on public administration. Subsequently, André W. Van Rest, Richard C. Kearney, and Stephen T. Smith finished the initial drafts. Direction of the work, the final editing of the manuscript, and the concluding stages of the manuscript preparation were the responsibilities of Hills.

We sincerely wish to thank Judy Van Rest for her willingness to undertake various editorial chores, and Judy Grove and Connie Campbell for their work in typing the manuscript.

This publication was supported in part by the Social and Rehabilitation Service, Department of Health, Education, and Welfare, Washington, D.C., Grant No. 15-P-55226/6.

Norman, Oklahoma   William G. Hills
January 15, 1975   André W. Van Rest
                                      Richard C. Kearney
                                      Stephen T. Smith

CONTENTS

Administration and Management

I. DEVELOPMENT, SCOPE, AND EMPHASIS

PUBLIC administrators have developed and administered public policies since man formed his first government thousands of years ago. The earliest known written record, the civil code of Hammurabi in ancient Sumer, dealt with the administration of property and contracts. Public administration as a formal area of study, however, did not emerge until the end of the nineteenth century. Traditionally, its origin is dated from the publication of Woodrow Wilson's essay "The Study of Public Administration" (1887). In this essay Wilson tried to illustrate the difference between politics and administration and at the same time to introduce the field of administrative studies to the American public. Wilson's essay led many early public administration scholars to think of politics and administration as mutually exclusive, and his call for efficient government anticipated the concerns of the scientific management movement.

The advent of the scientific management movement encouraged and coincided with the development of public administration as a special discipline. This movement emphasized the physiological factors in achieving work efficiency and gave much attention to the discovery of "principles" of administration. Frederick W. Taylor (1856–1915) is often called the father of scientific management. He and his followers, among them Frank B. Gilbreth, Henry Lawrence Gantt, and Harrington Emerson, attempted to measure by time-and-motion studies the activities of the manual worker in the factory and to discover ways of making the worker's efforts most productive. Taylor believed that scientific analysis would lead to the discovery of the "one best way" of performing a function. His ideas were introduced to government with the publication of his most famous work, *The Principles of Scientific Management* (1911). Henri Fayol (1841–1925), a brilliant French industrialist and perhaps the true father of modern management theory, laid down fourteen principles of administration which the manager should take into account: (1) division of work, (2) authority, (3) discipline, (4) unity of command, (5) unity of direction, (6) subordination of individual to general interest, (7) remuneration, (8) centralization, (9) scalar chain, (10) order, (11) equity, (12) stability of tenure, (13) initiative, and (14) esprit de corps. He then identified five elements of management: (1) planning, (2) organizing, (3) commanding, (4) coordinating, and (5) controlling. Fayol's best-known work, *General and Industrial Management*, was published in France in 1916, but it was not until 1929 that it was translated into English and not until 1949 that it was printed in the United States.

In the meantime the "principles" approach was effectively presented in the United States by James Mooney and Allan Reiley in their book *Onward Industry* (1931). This approach, however, was repudiated by Herbert Simon in his *Administrative Behavior* (1945). Simon demonstrated that the so-called principles of administration were at best proverbs, were ambiguous, and could lead to opposing conclusions. The fundamental concepts of Fayolism and Taylorism significantly influenced the thinking of early scholars in public administration and are still a part of the literature of administration and management.

During the Great Depression and World War II there was a significant expansion of governmental activities. The growth of government gave impetus to a new administrative school of thought, which reintroduced politics into the study of public administration. Because of the size of the government, public administrators became policy makers, and value judgments, pressure groups, conflict, power, and interpersonal relations became important concerns in the study of public administration.

The human relations movement replaced the preoccupation with formal authority relationships and organizational charts with a concern for organizations as social systems. The scientific examination of the human factor within organizations dates back to the Hawthorne experiments (1927–32). Elton Mayo and Fritz Roethlisberger showed that the informal organization could be as important to efficiency and productivity as rest periods, lighting, and monetary rewards. Although before the 1940's behavioral scientists were not deeply involved in the problems of administration and management, since that time their contributions to the field have been extensive. Sociologists Philip Selznick, Daniel Katz, and Alfred Kahn and others have contributed much to the understanding of organizations through their studies of culture, status, conflict, and other group-related factors. Psychologists Douglas McGregor, Rensis Likert, Chris Argyris, Fred E. Fiedler, and others have likewise contributed to the study of administration in their work on the nature of leadership, motivation, perception, and individual behavior.

Much knowledge is to be gained from the successes and failures of earlier administrators. To help the administrator of the 1970's draw upon the wealth of his predecessors' experiences and to give him an idea of the lines along which his profession has developed, we have included historical books in this section of the book. To provide a broad overview of public administration, its basic functions, and the state of the craft today, we have reviewed some introductory works on administration in both the public and the private domain. Finally, since much of the literature of public administration is devoted to such specific fields as public health administration, social work administration, and hospital and police administration, we have included several books that are directly concerned with these areas and yet are general enough to be of value to all practicing administrators.

Blum, Henrick L., and Alvin R. Leonard. *Public Administration—A Public Health Viewpoint.* New York, Macmillan Company, 1963. 532 pp.

Based on the philosophy that democracy demands a purpose of its public agencies, this book examines some major areas of administrative decision making in the public health field. It provides practical advice on submitting budgets, making promotions and evaluations, initiating research and training programs, developing legislation relating to professional societies and voluntary agencies, and testifying at public hearings.

The authors first develop a working model of democracy and discuss the responsibility of the public agency in carrying out the public will. They then describe the relationship between the public health agency and the general public, special-interest groups, and certain peer groups and take a look at policy making and program development in the health field. Finally, while considering the organizational aspects of public health administration, they examine the formal and informal relationships within a public agency and discuss such topics as employee interests, participation in unions, loyalty, training, chain of command, delegation, span of control, hierarchy, authority, supervision, and communication.

Buechner, John C. *Public Administration*. Belmont, Calif., Dickenson Publishing Company, Inc., 1968. 114 pp.

Because of its conciseness, this book is of special value to the administrator. Buechner emphasizes public administration as a study, a process, and a vocation at all levels of government. After developing a framework for understanding public administration, he discusses organizational theory, bureaucracy, and fiscal administration. Although his focus is on public administration in American government, he also examines administrative systems in general. He considers the problems of comparing administrative systems, methods for comparison, and the various comparative models and theories. A bibliographical essay serves as a guide to further reading.

Dimock, Marshall E., and Gladys Ogden Dimock. *Public Administration*. 4th ed. New York, Holt, Rinehart and Winston, Inc., 1969. 634 pp.

This introduction to public administration presents the theory and the structure of public administration. The authors believe that public administration, in response to deep social needs, has become more comparative, behavioral, economic, and political. Though public administration has drawn on all the social sciences in recent times, the discipline has maintained a core of theory and practice that is peculiarly its own and is most closely related to political theory. The interdependent nature of public policy and public administration is emphasized. The human aspects of administration and the programmatic aspects of government with its relationship to the economy are stressed. The book maintains a comparative theme dealing with administration in other countries, development administration, business management, and government practice. The chapters are organized into four parts, dealing with the broader environment of organization, institutions, and forces in public administration today; personnel and manpower systems; the management of government programs; and the economic and financial aspects of public programs.

Gatherer, A., and M. D. Warren, eds. *Management and the Health Services.* New York, Pergamon Press, Inc., 1971. 176 pp.

This collection of papers deals with a number of subjects in the area of health-services administration and management. They concentrate on the National Health Service in Britain, but most of the articles have universal relevance.

The trends in society that have had a major impact on health and health services are discussed, along with such considerations as management's place in an industrial society, managerial functions and skills, new theories in management, and the use of the analytical approach to decision making. Other papers relate the development of health services to data collection, planning, evaluation, operational research, and personnel selection.

The last two papers examine the contributions of sociology to medical administration and view the tasks of the community physician, epidemiologist, and community counselor in relation to changes in medical needs, clinical practice, and prevention of disease.

Gladden, E.N. *A History of Public Administration.* 2 vols. Vol. I. *From the Earliest Times to the Eleventh Century.* 269 pp. Vol. II. *From the Eleventh Century to the Present Day.* 420 pp. London, Frank Cass, 1972.

This comprehensive history of public administration emphasizes three major characteristics of public administration: continuity, universality, and subordination to the policy decisions of political leadership.

Volume I surveys the profession, from the prehistoric cave dwellers to the major civilizations of ancient Egypt, the Mediterranean city-states, Imperial Rome, early India and China, Byzantium, and the West to A.D. 1000. The material is derived from archaeology, oral traditions, early writing, and contemporary primitive societies. Volume II extends the scope of the investigation to pre-Columbian America, medieval and sixteenth-century Europe, and more recent administration in China and India. Four modern systems of public administration are treated: Anglo-Saxon, colonial, Russian, and international. Consideration is given to the adaptation of public administration to the needs of today and those of the future.

Gulick, Luther, and Lyndall Urwick, eds. *Papers on the Science of Administration*. New York, Institute of Public Administration, Columbia University, 1937. 196 pp.

This book is a collection of papers by outstanding pioneers in the field of administration. The editors collected the papers to make readily available important contributions in the administrative field that previously had not been widely circulated. In addition to the editors themselves, noted contributors include Henri Fayol, James D. Mooney, and Mary Parker Follett.

Haiman, Theo, and William G. Scott. *Management in the Modern Organization*. Boston, Houghton Mifflin Company, 1970. 604 pp.

This work combines the principal functions of management with the contributions of the behavioral sciences and the concepts of systems and process. Within the systems framework management is defined as a social and technical process that utilizes resources, influences human actions, and facilitates changes in order to accomplish organization goals. The primary functions of management are identified as planning, organizing, staffing, influencing, and controlling. Management is viewed as a system, insofar as it consists of inputs, outputs, and the processes that connect them and permit feedback. Using the functional-systems approach, the authors incorporate into the management system various inputs from the behavioral sciences—particularly from sociology and psychology—such as leadership, motivation, and group dynamics. Quantitative tools and techniques, operations research, PERT, matrix organization, and normative decision theory are considered part of the over-all concept of the management system. Part I discusses the nature, environment, and evolution of management. Part II considers decision making and communication as processes linking the five managerial functions. These linking processes govern the flow of organizational resources. Parts III through VII examine the managerial functions. In conclusion, the authors illustrate with nine examples the interdisciplinary nature of the theory and principles covered in the book.

Henderson, Keith M. *Emerging Synthesis in American Public Administration*. New York, Asia Publishing House, 1966. 72 pp.

This book, a chronological study of the literature of American public administration, is concerned with those works relevant to the discipline in tracing the evolution and current status of the study of public administration. The analysis of the historical emphasis in administrative thought is developed within the categories thesis (1887–1945, structural), antithesis (1945–1958, behavioral and environmental), and synthesis (since 1958, organizational systems). Comparative public administration is followed through the bureaucratic-system approach, the input-output approach, and the component approach. The field of development administration is briefly surveyed with respect to the Middle East, Africa, Asia, and Latin America.

Hills, William G., Voyle C. Scurlock, Harold D. Viaille, and James A. West, eds. *Conducting the People's Business: The Framework and Functions of Public Administration.* Norman, University of Oklahoma Press, 1973. 506 pp.

This collection of sixty-two articles concentrates on the problems and practice of applied management and is written with the practicing manager in mind. It should be especially useful to the manager promoted from the ranks of the specialist practitioner. Technical terminology and jargon are minimized in the articles. Many of the articles were selected from smaller publications that the manager normally might not see, with an emphasis on material useful to state and local government, and human-resources administrators.

Part One is a general introduction to the problems and practices of public administration. Part Two deals with elements of the administrative process: planning, organizing, developing and directing human resources, and controlling. Part Three examines the role of individuals and unions in changing ideas about bureaucracy.

Koontz, Harold, and Cyril O'Donnell. *Principles of Management: An Analysis of Managerial Functions.* 5th ed. New York, McGraw-Hill Book Company, 748 pp.

This introductory work presents a sound conceptual framework of fundamental knowledge in the management field. Management activities are regarded as ongoing processes in which every manager, in order to achieve organization objectives, is involved.

The book is organized according to management functions: planning, organizing, staffing, directing, and controlling. A survey of the different schools of management is provided in the chapter on management analysis. The advanced techniques of planning and control (or PERT) are discussed. The contributions of behavioral scientists to management are stressed.

Lepawsky, Albert. *Administration: The Art and Science of Organization and Management.* New York, Alfred A. Knopf, Inc., 1949. 670 pp.

A classic collection of readings on administration, presented, in part, to help the reader "develop an appreciation of sound and tested administrative methods, managerial techniques, and organizational devices." The readings are organized around three major subjects—the art of administration, the science of organization, and the technique of management. A broad range of classical, historical, and contemporary ideas is presented in the works of such diverse writers as Henri Fayol, Brooks Adams, Charles A. Beard, Luther Gulick, Woodrow Wilson, Max Weber, Pericles, Frederick W. Taylor, Adolf Hitler, Thorsten Veblen, Leo Tolstoy, Marshall Dimock, Joseph Stalin, and Dwight Waldo.

Merrill, Harwood Ferry, ed. *Classics in Management: Selections from the Historic Literature of Management.* New York, American Management Association, Inc., 1960. 446 pp.

This work affords the reader an opportunity to acquaint himself with the works of sixteen of the "old masters" and to explore their ideas. The reader is provided with selections from masterpieces in management literature, beginning with an address by Robert Owen in 1813 and concluding with excerpts from the work of Elton Mayo, published in 1945. Included are the writings of such authors as Charles Babbage, Frederick W. Taylor, Henry Lawrence Gantt, Harrington Emerson, Henri Fayol, and Mary Parker Follett.

Metcalf, Henry C., and Lyndall Urwick, eds. *Dynamic Administration: The Collected Papers of Mary Parker Follett.* New York, Harper and Brothers, 1942. 320 pp.

Miss Follett was a remarkable woman who was well known

on both sides of the Atlantic as a social scientist and philosopher. Her earliest interests, at the turn of the century, were education and vocational guidance, but her principal effort shifted from political and social issues to problems of organization and industrial relations.

These fourteen papers, all delivered between 1925 and 1932, relate to the scientific foundations of management. They include such interrelated subjects as constructive conflict, the giving of orders, power, and leader and expert.

She viewed the fundamental bases of management as psychological and summarized her thinking in four basic principles of organization and administration: (1) coordination by direct contact with the persons responsible, (2) coordination in the early stages, (3) coordination as the reciprocal relating of all factors in a situation, and (4) coordination as a continuing process. The heart of these principles is coordination, of course, and the goal is control.

Pfiffner, John M., and Robert Presthus. *Public Administration*. 5th ed. New York, Ronald Press, 1967. 568 pp.

An introduction to public administration dealing with the environment of public administration, functions of the administrator, organization, personnel administration, financial administration, administrative law and reputation, and administrative responsibility. The bargaining phase of the public sector is stressed, particularly the separation-of-powers system, which forces public officials to play a political role in order to achieve the support necessary for their programs. The authors also discuss the specialist role of higher administrators, the utility of behavioral research, and the use of computer techniques and quantitative controls.

Rakich, Jonathan. *Hospital Organization and Management*. St. Louis, Catholic Hospital Association, 1972. 300 pp.

A collection of classic, current, and controversial readings on the hospital organization and its management. Particular emphasis is given to organization, personnel management, labor relations, decision making, planning, and social responsibility. Part I, the major section of the book, deals with the hospital as a functioning organization, that is, a humanitarian, quasi-bureaucratic, quasi-authoritarian organization with a mission of patient care. This section considers the hospital's organizational structure, the function and responsibilities of the board of trustees, the evolving professional role of the hospital administrator, and the functions and responsibilities of the medical staff through a systems analysis. Other areas covered are hospital-employee motivation, supervision and leadership in a hospital setting, federal labor legislation as it pertains to the hospital industry, the effects of unions on hospital management, operations research, and decision making.

A final section deals with several health-care issues and trends. Hospital responsibility is discussed from an internal and an external point of view. The importance of planning, both within and among health-care institutions, is stressed as a prerequisite for the efficient operation and allocation of resources. The last two readings are critical examinations of health-care delivery and financing systems.

Schatz, Harry A., ed. *Social Work Administration: A Resource Book*. New York, Council on Social Work Education, 1970. 398 pp.

Many social program administrators have risen from the ranks. The practitioner is often unprepared to assume an administrative role. This book of readings is intended to help prepare the practitioner-turned-administrator for his new tasks in the field of social work. It is meant to be used for individual study or for agency in-service training programs. The material is arranged in six sections: an overview of social work administration, organizational structure, administrative processes, man-in-administration, environment, and budget and finance. The bibliography is arranged under the same topics.

Sheldon, Oliver. *The Philosophy of Management.* New York, Pitman Publishing Corporation, 1965. 296 pp.

This classic in management literature first appeared in 1924. The author discusses some of the fundamental concepts in management, such as the impact of environment— market, economy, and governmental attitudes and action— on individual concerns and business in general: the relationship of science and management; and management as a profession. Sheldon's philosophy of management: a firm should provide goods and services in whatever volume required for the least possible price compatible with adequate quality, distributed in such a manner that the highest ends of the community are promoted.

Waldo, Dwight. *The Novelist on Organization and Administration: An Inquiry into the Relationship Between Two Worlds.* Berkeley, Institute of Governmental Studies, 1968. 158 pp.

An "administrative novel" is one in which an organization is essential to the story, significantly affecting the character's activities. Waldo's view is that the student or practitioner of administration can obtain from the administrative novel better knowledge of himself, both personally and professionally, and of his job.

The novelist also has much to learn from the student of administration and organization. In the past the novelist has tended to avoid the world of administration or has given a shallow and distorted view of it. Waldo believes that the novelist and the administrative scientist can reach a mutual understanding if the novelist can be persuaded to write about the central problems of organizational life, guided by research on organizations and administration.

The book includes 154 reviews of administrative novels that can be used as learning resources.

Wilson, D. W., and Roy C. McLaren. *Police Administration.* 3d ed. New York, McGraw-Hill Book Company, 1972. 742 pp.

This book discusses police responsibility to the community and society and police relationships with other agencies and with local, state, and federal governments. The authors describe management problems in the police department and urge the use of evaluation in efforts to improve administrative procedures. Principles of police organizational structure are presented, and the need for better leadership and supervision is emphasized.

A section of the book is devoted to the administration of police field operations, including the broad areas of patrol, investigation, traffic control and enforcement, and crime prevention. Information is presented for the administration of a police department's auxiliary and technical services (the crime lab, the prison, property, and equipment). Appendices contain sample reports and forms, training materials, and other information useful to the police administrator.

Wren, Daniel A. *The Evolution of Management Thought.* New York, Ronald Press, 1972. 556 pp.

This book traces the evolution of management thought from its earliest days to the present by examining the backgrounds, ideas, and influence of the major contributors. The significant development and trends in management thought are outlined chronologically with illustrations of how environmental forces—economic, social, and political institutions and values—shaped the development of management ideas. Wren provides useful charts summarizing the major directions of management thinking. The work is devoted to contributors from the mainstreams of management thought in a text book format designed for classroom use. Also very helpful is Claude S. George. *The History of Management Thought* (Englewood Cliffs, N. J., Prentice-Hall, Inc., 2d ed. 1972, 224 pp.). It deals with the same topic, but its perspective and shorter length should make it particularly useful and interesting to the practicing manager. Although shorter than Wren's volume, George's book provides solid background, information, and insights for the more casual student of management literature.

II. THE ORGANIZATION

WE live in a society dominated by deliberately planned organizations with specific goals. Organizations allow the achievement of goals that are beyond the capabilities of a single individual. Ours is truly an "organizational society": we are born in hospitals, educated in schools and universities for organizational employment elsewhere, and buried by funeral organizations. Day-to-day survival depends on organizations that supply us with food, electricity, and paychecks. The principle cause of our increasing dependence on organizations is our technological society, which requires specialized groups of people to perform increasingly complex tasks.

To operate an organization effectively and efficiently, managers must solve problems involving the following elements: structure, people, and change. Organization theory deals with the structural element. An organization, deliberately planned and having specific goals, must establish means of coordinating the activities of people to achieve those goals. This requires a formal framework, setting limits within which management can operate. Max Weber, an important theorist of the formal organization, formulated an ideal structure that emphasized rationality and logic to maximize the organization's effectiveness, efficiency, and productivity. The formal structure is developed to increase stability in human relationships by reducing uncertainties about the nature of the systems' structure and the human roles in it. Power and authority relationships are clearly defined; work is divided and assigned to officeholders, not persons; and rules and regulations are written down and formalized to produce impersonal decisions. Weber called the structure of formal relationships the bureaucracy, and from it we have the useful ideas of hierarchy, line and staff divisions, and centralized control.

The concept of the formal organization is limited because, however rational and logical it may be, situations arise that are not anticipated by the rules and regulations. People in the organization invent informal solutions and relationships, and these unofficial practices become important guides for controlling the organization. The famous studies at Western Electric's Hawthorne plant have shown how extensive and influential this informal organization is. The informal organization not only controlled unanticipated situations but also set unofficial norms regulating performance, behavior, and productivity.

The need for integrating the formal and informal theories of organizational structure is great. Although important contributions have been made from many academic disciplines, no single or entirely satisfactory theory has yet emerged. The bibliography includes a representative sample of the best thinking in the field.

It has been said that the only problem with organizations is that there are people in them. Knowledge of people and their behavior is the second important element in the effective and efficient management of an organization. When the goals of the organization and the goals of the individual are not compatible, behavior emerges that is neither anticipated nor required by the organization's rational design. This unanticipated behavior can have costly consequences for both the individual and the organization.

Managing human behavior in an organizational setting is a complicated business. Action-oriented practitioners demand answers to complex problems with a degree of precision that is beyond existing knowledge. The behavioral sciences, in turn, are confounded by the influence of values on what can be studied, what can be manipulated or changed, and what will be accepted. Organizational behavior includes such complex factors as the motivation and perception of the individual, the social processes of small groups, and the effects of organizational determinants (such as power and authority) on both the individual and the group. The selections in Section IIA below provide the administrator with a working knowledge of behavioral variables in the organizational environment, and illustrate the application of behavioral science to the management of people.

Organization development (OD) deals with the elements of change that confront managers in the efficient and effective operation of their organizations. It is based upon the premise that men do not have to respond passively or negatively to change but can plan organizational changes to release the creative abilities and skills of the members. Organization development uses a variety of methods designed to change skills, attitudes, behavior, and structures, with the aim of making the organization more adaptable and flexible by integrating the goals of the individual and the organization.

A. Organization Theory

Barnard, Chester I. *The Functions of the Executive*. Cambridge, Mass., Harvard University Press, 1938. 334 pp.

This book is a pivotal work in management literature. A skillful practitioner and intelligent student of management—Barnard was president of the New Jersey Bell Telephone Company when he wrote the book—the author found the existing organization theories and the emerging studies of the social scientists inaccurate and confusing. For Barnard, earlier works dealt only with the superficialities of organization—its topography and cartography—because they concentrated on the origin and nature of authority and assumed that human behavior is explained in terms of "economic man." Barnard's observation of skilled executives and his own experience led him to search for the universals of organization and to develop a more nearly complete statement of the executive process.

The first part of this book constitutes the theoretical substructure: knowledge from the social sciences is compressed and expressed in terms of organization. The physical, psychological, and social factors of cooperative systems are described; formal and informal organizations are defined and their relationships shown.

The second part, based on Barnard's experience, deals with the behavior of organizations and of the people in them, especially executives. All organizations require persons who are able to communicate and willing to contribute their efforts toward the accomplishment of a common purpose. These requirements also identify the essential executive functions: to provide a system of communication, to promote the securing of essential efforts, and to formulate and define purpose. Barnard concludes with a declaration of faith:

I believe in the power of the cooperation of men of free will to make men free to cooperate. . . . I believe that the expansion of cooperation and the development of the individual are mutually dependent realities, and that a due proportion or balance between them is a necessary condition of human welfare.

Blau, Peter M., and W. Richard Scott. *Formal Organizations: A Comparative Approach.* San Francisco, Chandler Publishing Company, 1962. 312 pp.

This book is an introduction to the study of formal organizations. The authors place primary emphasis on the analysis of empirical data. A classification scheme of formal organizations is developed on the basis of the recipient, or "prime beneficiary," of the organization's activity. Four kinds of formal organizations are identified: mutual-benefit associations (whose prime beneficiary is the rank-and-file membership), business enterprises (whose prime beneficiary is the owner), service organizations (in which the client population is the prime beneficiary), and commonweal organizations (which primarily benefit the general public). A chapter on the organization and the publics and the frequent references to two welfare organizations studied by the authors give this book added relevance.

The social structure of work groups is examined with regard to such aspects of informal organizations as norms, cohesion, and informal status. Supervision is seen as a major factor affecting work groups, and worker productivity is related to the degree of loyalty and support the workers give to their supervisors. Conflict between staff and line and the ensuing power struggle among managers are discussed. Impersonal mechanisms of control are compared and contrasted with hierarchical directives.

Subsequent chapters deal with communication, supervision, managerial control, relationships of organizations to their environments, and organizational change. The book concludes with a forty-three-page annotated bibliography classifying some eight hundred items.

Carzo, Rocco, Jr., and John N. Yanouzas. *Formal Organization: A Systems Approach.* Homewood, Ill., Richard D. Irwin, Inc., 1967. 592 pp.

The authors use the traditional, or classical, frame of reference to show the nature of formal organization and a systems approach to explain organizational design. Some primary concepts of traditional theory are departmentation, unity of command, span of management, and organizational authority. Behavior patterns in organizational life are dealt with in sections on informal organizations, dysfunctions of formal organization, line-and-staff conflicts, power structure, and power struggle in organizations.

In organizational design each component activity is viewed as a subsystem of a total system. Various kinds of systems are described, and a general model of system reliability is given. Uses of the Markov chain analysis and the waiting-line theory for formulating organizational design are discussed.

Liberal use is made of examples, case studies, and models to illustrate concepts of systems design and systems operations.

Etzioni, Amitai. *Modern Organizations.* Englewood Cliffs, N.J., Prentice-Hall, Inc., 1964. 192 pp.

An introductory overview of organization theory. Defining organizations as "social units which are deliberately constructed to seek specific goals," the author focuses on organizational goals, structure, and environment.

Etzioni traces the synthesis of the formal, or scientific management, school, and the informal, or human relations, school, into a new structuralist approach to the study of organizations. A succinct summary of Taylorism and the Hawthorne experiments is included, along with an examination of Max Weber's works as representative of early structuralist thought. The author describes the problems of organizational control and leadership and the uses of coercive, utilitarian, and normative power. The role of administrators and professionals in positions of authority in professional, semiprofessional, and service organizations is discussed. Organizational conflict, such as the strain between personal needs and the organization's goals, is seen as a problem that cannot be eliminated. Not all conflict is bad; indeed, some degree of conflict is necessary for a healthy organization. The book concludes with an analysis of the relations between organizations and their clients and between organizations and their larger social environment.

Fayol, Henri. *General and Industrial Management.* Tr. by Constance Storrs. London, Pitman Publishing Corporation, 1949. 110 pp.

Written by the first comprehensive theorist of modern times, this book was originally published in France in 1916. Henri Fayol, a distinguished French engineer and administrator, was a universalist who believed that there is a single "administrative science" whose principles could be applied with equal validity to the management of business and industrial enterprises or to the management of governmental agencies.

Fayol identified and described five functions of administration: planning, organizing (men and materials), commanding, coordinating, and controlling; and formulated several principles that are well known today: authority should not be conceived apart from responsibility, unity of command and unity of direction should exist, initiative and esprit de corps must exist.

Gross, Bertram M. *The Managing of Organizations: The Administrative Struggle.* 2 vols. New York, Free Press, 1964. 972 pp.

A major work wherein the author synthesizes the chief concepts necessary to an analysis of the structure and performance of various organizations in their actual environments.

Early chapters contain the historical, philosophical, and social background of both administrative theory and the "administrative revolution." After dealing with the management of organizations, the conflict-cooperation nexus, the power-authority-responsibility triangle, and both the immediate and the general environment, Gross turns to structure. In this section he discusses the "human beings" as individuals, and the formal and informal aspects of people-in-organizations.

The remainder of the work is devoted to a consideration of performance. To facilitate an understanding of organizational performance, Gross has developed a conceptual scheme, which he calls a global matrix of organizational purposes. This matrix consists of seven dimensions of organizational purpose: the satisfaction of various interests, output of services or goods, efficiency or profitability, investment in organizational viability, mobilization of resources, observance of codes, and technical or administrative rationality. Management is presented as an integrating process that involves making decisions under conditions of uncertainty, communicating imperfect information through multiple channels, and engaging in endless rounds of planning, activating, and evaluating.

A comprehensive bibliography enhances the value of this work. (A condensed, one-volume edition of this monumental study was published in 1968 under the title *Organizations and Their Managing*; it differs principally in the exclusion of the historical material on administrative thought.)

Jun, Jong S., and William B. Storm, eds. *Tomorrow's Organizations: Challenges and Strategies*. Glenview, Ill., Scott, Foresman and Company, 1973. 450 pp.

Jun and Storm believe that there is a need for a different kind of organization with new values, methods, and structures. To develop an organization capable of dealing effectively with contemporary and future problems, the authors advocate the integration of various organization theories to create new methods for solving organizational problems. The papers presented in this volume were selected to show how three perspectives could be joined in an integrative approach to tomorrow's organizations: micro (human capabilities and behavior in the organization); macro (a holistic, or total-systems, approach); and phenomenological (concerned with such things as human behavior and individual perceptions of reality).

The four major parts of this work are entitled "The Different Future," "New Dimensions for Tomorrow's Organizations," "New Perspectives in Organizational Theory," and "Strategies for a Changing Organization." Each is preceded by a lengthy introduction. Authors of the thirty-seven selections include such recognized scholars as Herman Kahn, Jay W. Lorsh, William G. Scott, Chris Argyris, Warren Bennis, Edgar Schein, Robert Blake, Amitai Etzioni, Peter Blau, Victor A. Thompson, and Scott Greer.

Koontz, Harold, ed. *Toward a Unified Theory of Management: A Symposium*. New York, McGraw-Hill Book Company, 1964. 274 pp.

This book resulted from a management symposium held for the purpose of reaching some general agreement on management theories and to determine whether it might be possible to develop a unified theory of management. Koontz includes eleven of the papers presented at the symposium, together with excerpts from the general discussions by prominent academicians and managers who were in attendance at the symposium.

The first chapter is a reprint of Koontz's earlier article in the *Harvard Business Review*, in which he describes six "schools of management": management process, empirical, human behavioral, social systems, decision theory, and mathematical. Koontz does not recommend any one school, preferring an eclectic approach to management theory. The final chapter is Koontz's summary of the symposium.

Lawrence, Paul R., and Jay W. Lorsch. *Organization and Environment: Managing Differentiation and Integration.* Homewood, Ill., Richard D. Irwin, Inc., 1969. 280 pp.

Emphasizing that there is no one best way to organize, Lawrence and Lorsch advance a contingency theory of organization. Basing their conclusion on a study of ten firms in three industries, the authors conclude that the appropriate degree of departmental differentiation (specialization) and integration (coordination) depends on the certainty of the environment in which the department exists. The classical, bureaucratic form of organization was found to be most effective for firms in stable environments, while the modern human relations organization was most effective for firms in uncertain environments. The impact of environmental attributes is further related to coordinative mechanisms, modes of conflict resolution, formality of structure, interpersonal orientation, management-time orientation, and departmental-goal orientation.

The book provides a good summary of classical, human relations, and contingency organizational theory. By relegating most of their methodological work to an appendix, the authors keep the presentation of their research data, and the resulting theory, nontechnical and readable.

Leavitt, Harold J., William R. Dill, and Henry B. Eyring. *The Organizational World.* New York, Harcourt Brace Jovanovich, Inc., 1973. 336 pp.

A description of organizations and how they work, based on the assumption that organizations are both a necessity and the single best vehicle for social change. The authors stress that organizations do exist and will continue to exist and that people should learn how to make them work better. A systems approach is explicit throughout the work: organizations and their components—goals, structure, technology, and people—are seen as dynamic and interacting.

The authors offer general guidance for managers in such

areas as job specialization, management information systems, computers, conflict, organization growth, client relations, the organization abroad, and organizational and human change. The book provides an interesting introduction to the world of organizations and should serve as excellent material for public administration and management training programs.

Mouzelis, Nicos P. *Organization and Bureaucracy: An Analysis of Modern Theories.* Chicago, Aldine Publishing Company, 1967. 230 pp.

An overview of the major theories of organization with special emphasis given to two major traditions in the study of organizations: the bureaucratic and the managerial.

The bureaucratic school originated with the works of Karl Marx, Max Weber, and Robert Michels. The theories of each are analyzed, with particular emphasis on Weber's "ideal" bureaucracy. The managerial tradition has its roots in the scientific management school of Frederick Taylor. Mouzelis traces subsequent developments of this tradition through the search for universal principles of management, the human relations movement, and the decision-making approach of Herbert Simon.

The author notes that a convergence of the two major traditions is found in recent works that employ a structural approach to organizations. These studies have been primarily concerned with the organization as a system and the roles of conflict and power in the organizational setting. Mouzelis calls for greater sociological emphasis in the study of organizations and urges development of more general theory and more cross-cultural, historical studies of various organizations.

Peabody, Robert L. *Organizational Authority: Superior-Subordinate Relationships in Three Public Service Organizations.* New York, Atherton Press, 1964. 163 pp.

This work derives from the study of authority relationships in three public service organizations: an elementary school, the branch office of a public welfare agency, and a municipal police department. These organizations reflect variations in the exercise of functional authority based on technical competence, personal skills, and influence, as contrasted to formal authority based on legitimacy and the rewards and sanctions inherent in a person's position.

Both kinds of authority are necessary to achieve objectives and goals, as well as to satisfy an individual's needs through his participation in organizational activities. Authority relationships are basic to the achievement of organizational goals, but conflicting attitudes toward authority constitute a major source of tension within an organization.

Perrow, Charles. *Organizational Analysis: A Sociological View*. Belmont, Calif., and London, Brooks/Cole, Tavistock, 1970. 192 pp.

Perrow presents a structural perspective of organization. He uses this approach because, in his opinion, most organizational problems result from faulty organizational structure, rather than from the personalities or individual characteristics of employees.

Bureaucratic structure is examined as a form all organizations strive to attain because they require specialization, control over extraorganizational factors influencing employees, and maximum stabilization of their environment. Some organizations, however, such as research institutions, are best structured on a nonbureaucratic model because their procedures are not routine and the nature of their technologies changes. The strong influence of a firm's technology leads Perrow to offer a typology of organizations based on the kind of work they do: craft, nonroutine, engineering, and routine—a continuum reaching from the nonbureaucratic to the strongly bureaucratic form.

Relationships between the organization and its environment are also considered, including the issues of organizational legitimacy, co-optation, cultural setting, other organizations, and politics. Finally, the book stresses organizational goal analysis as the method offering the most nearly complete understanding of an organization and the best clue to organizational character. Four kinds of goals are explored: output, system, product, and derived.

Perrow concludes that there is not one best way of managing all organizations, nor one best kind of goal for all organizations to pursue.

Pfiffner, John M., and Frank P. Sherwood. *Administrative Organization.* Englewood Cliffs, N.J., Prentice-Hall, Inc., 1960. 482 pp.

In uniting the traditional and behavioral approaches to the study of organizations, the authors superimpose upon the conventional job-task pyramid five overlays reflecting social processes that affect the formal lines of interaction: (1) the sociometric overlay primarily consists of the contacts people have with each other because of personal attraction, (2) the functional overlay arises out of relationships created by technical experts who exercise authority because of their knowledge and skills, (3) the decision overlay manifests itself when the flow of significant decisions does not correspond to the structure of the formal hierarchy, (4) the power overlay concerns the presence of power centers that do not coincide with the official structure of authority, and (5) the communication overlay involves the entire process by which information and perceptions are transmitted throughout the organization.

The totality of these overlays exemplifies the complexity of organization. This complexity is further illustrated by the authors' discussion of goal systems which operate within the organization, partially coinciding with its formal aims and partially modifying its formal structure.

Presthus, Robert. *The Organizational Society: An Analysis and a Theory.* New York, Alfred A. Knopf, Inc., 1962. 324 pp.

In this interdisciplinary study of large-scale organizations and the pressures and influences they exert on behavior and values, Presthus views the large organization as a miniature society exercising a major disciplinary force on the people who work in it by imposing its bureaucratic values on the individual. The individual conforms to this organizational dictatorship of norms to avoid anxiety.

There are three types of personal accommodation to the demands of the organization: the authoritarian "upward-mobile" conforms to the bureaucratic ideology; the "indifferent" refuses to compete for bureaucratic rewards, preferring to seek satisfaction elsewhere; the "ambivalent" is found somewhere in between, suffering from a schizoid desire for bureaucratic rewards and status and a concomitant rejection of the bureaucratic values.

The author then discusses certain dysfunctional social effects of the large-scale organization, which he feels have resulted in a challenge to America's hegemony in technology and economic growth. He concludes by showing the necessity for conflict and continuing change within the organization in order for it to provide a more beneficial influence on those who work within it and on society as a whole.

Thayer, Frederick C. *An End to Hierarchy! An End to Competition! Organizing the Politics and Economics of Survival.* New York, New Viewpoints, 1973. 232 pp.

Thayer argues that a revolutionary transformation is taking place in organizations, one that is as important as any revolution ever recorded. The revolution is based on new techniques of small-group decision making that seek to build consensus by dealing directly and democratically with conflict. Among the examples of this trend, Thayer lists Organization Development (OD), which stresses collaborative teamwork, and participative management, which seeks to democratize decisions at low levels of the hierarchy. But consensual decision making works only if no outside individual or group has the power to impose a decision. Two major impediments to the nonauthoritarian revolution are conventional political and economic theories, particularly organizational hierarchy and the ethic of competition.

Thayer sees hierarchy as the fundamental cause of alienation and competition as a failure even on its home territory—the economic marketplace. The solution requires a restructuring of belief, which will depart from a single-minded emphasis on the individual, and stress the creative act of building consensus as the primary act of citizenship, thereby putting an end to destructive hierarchical relationships and competition.

Weber, Max. *The Theory of Social and Economic Organization.* Ed. by Talcott Parsons, tr. by A. M. Henderson and Talcott Parsons. 2d ed. Glencoe, Ill., The Free Press, 1957. 436 pp.

This sociological analysis of bureaucracy is a classic work to which all subsequent scholars in the field of public administration are indebted.

Weber regards bureaucracy as the most efficient form of administrative organization, primarily because experience and expertise are required to make technical decisions. Furthermore, the discipline exacted by the rules and coordination of hierarchical authority promotes rational and consistent pursuit of organizational objectives.

An analysis of formal organization is derived from the examination of authority structures present within organizations. Three kinds of authority are identified and discussed: traditional, charismatic, and legal.

Weber's theory of bureaucracy is based on five characteristics of a bureaucratic organization: (1) organizational tasks distributed through various positions in the organization, implying a clear-cut division of labor; (2) positions organized into a hierarchical authority structure in the form of a pyramid, whereby the scope of the superior's authority is clearly defined; (3) a formal set of rules and regulations controlling the decision-making process of organization officers; (4) organization officers, who are usually impersonal in their transactions with fellow officers and clients of the organization; (5) organization employees, who are usually full time, regarding their employment with the organization as a career with set rules governing hiring, promotions, and transfers.

Woodward, Joan. *Industrial Organization: Theory and Practice*. London, Oxford University Press, 1965. 282 pp.

In examining one hundred diverse British firms, Woodward attempted to discern similarities and differences among the most successful and least successful organizations. The only direct relationship found was that firms with similar administrative structures had similar production systems, indicating that the imperatives of a firm's technology had the greatest effect on that firm's administrative structure. The most successful firms were those whose administrative characteristics best reflected the demands of their production systems.

The book is considered controversial because Woodward's research questions the usefulness of applying the classic principles of management to the administrative structure of a firm. Firms whose organizational structure reflected the classic principles were not always judged the most successful.

B. Organization Behavior

Blumberg, Paul. *Industrial Democracy: The Sociology of Participation*. New York, Schocken Books, 1969. 278 pp.

This book offers the reader a basic understanding of the theory and application of workers' participation in the decision-making process in business and industry.

After developing a novel interpretation of the classic Hawthorne experiments at Western Electric, Blumberg reviews various empirical studies of worker participation. Hugh Clegg's influential theory of worker management through the trade union is refuted. The author then develops his thesis that worker participation is a means of alleviating labor alienation in modern industry, even though the work tasks and processes remain unchanged. The book concludes with an analysis of the philosophical basis and application of worker's management in Yugoslavia.

Gawthrop, Louis C. *Bureaucratic Behavior in the Executive Branch*. New York, Free Press, 1969. 276 pp.

This volume deals with the ways in which the executive branch resolves its internal conflicts, makes decisions, develops a sense of loyalty within its ranks, and responds to the internal and external forces of change. Gawthrop's major premise is that conflict and decision making are integrally related to each other, directly related to the concept of organizational loyalty, and indirectly related to the concept of organizational change. He develops a systematic analysis of this premise and formulates an analytical model for explaining the functioning of bureaucratic systems by looking at the manner in which the executive branch is conditioned to respond to the inevitable demands for change, while comparing the analysis of the executive bureaucracy to a similar analysis of private organizations. Gawthrop explains the characteristics, advantages, and disadvantages of bureaucracy and deals with conflict, decision making, and loyalty in public and private bureaucracies. Using change as a conceptual framework for the study of bureaucratic behavior, he distinguishes between two kinds of change: consolidation and innovation. Consolidation is change induced by pressures from the external or internal environment solely within the context of existing organizational structures, if at all possible. It demonstrates a strong commitment toward moderation and compromise. Innovation is change initiated by administrators in a deliberate effort to search for improved performance programs. It emphasizes the need for identification of problems before they become overt. The author concludes that with the exception of the Defense Department, the Bureau of the Budget, and a few other agencies, consolidative behavior predominates in most federal agencies.

Hampton, David R., Charles E. Summer, and Ross A. Weber. *Organizational Behavior and the Practice of Management.* Rev. ed. Glenview, Ill., Scott, Foresman and Company, 1973. 940 pp.

The objective of this book is to give the reader an understanding of individual, interpersonal, and group behavior in organizations and help him see how this knowledge can be applied to the functions of management.

The authors present the theory and research of motivation, communication, influence, and human interaction and explore the possibilities for application of these theories and related research findings to the management functions of organizing, planning, controlling, leading, and rewarding. Special sections are devoted to the origin and management of conflict in organizations and to techniques of organizational development.

Each of the twelve chapters contains text material, case studies, and selected readings. Over all, the work constitutes a very useful review of the literature on organizational behavior.

Hersey, Paul, and Kenneth H. Blanchard. *Management of Organizational Behavior: Utilizing Human Resources.* 2d ed. Englewood Cliffs, N.J., Prentice-Hall, Inc., 1972. 210 pp.

This work utilizes behavioral science findings to develop a conceptual framework for understanding human behavior within the organizational setting. The authors begin with a discussion of human motives and needs, showing how they are satisfied and what they mean for the organization. Literature on leadership and motivation is reviewed, and the theories of Elton Mayo, Douglas McGregor, George C. Homans, Chris Argyris, Frederich Herzberg, and Rensis Likert are summarized. The authors conclude that the manager, to be most effective, must adapt his behavior to the situation. The book shows the manager how he can diagnose his personal needs and the demands of his followers, superiors, and associates, the organization, and the job itself. Behavioral-research findings are synthesized into what is termed the "life cycle theory of leadership," which encourages the manager to accommodate his style of leadership to the maturity of his followers. Processes and strategies for designing and implementing behavioral change are presented, with emphasis on the benefits of positive reinforcement.

Katz, Daniel, and Robert L. Kahn. *The Social Psychology of Organizations.* New York, John Wiley and Sons, 1966. 498 pp.

This pioneering work applies an open-systems approach to the study of behavior in large-scale organizations. The authors believe that the earlier approaches to organizational theory based on stereotyped organizational characteristics and on the identification of goals in terms of the purposes of the leaders have proved unsatisfactory. The approaches have been based on a closed system and thus fail to give proper consideration to the interactions between the organization and its environment. An open-systems theory is proposed as a better means of understanding the problems and processes of organizations. The authors illustrate the application of their theory in the areas of organization effectiveness, role behavior, power and authority, communications, policy making, decision making, leadership, and organizational change. The open-systems concepts of input, throughput, output, and feedback are recommended to place in perspective the organization and its environment.

Leavitt, Harold J. *Managerial Psychology: An Introduction to Individuals, Pairs and Groups in Organizations.* 3d ed. Chicago, University of Chicago Press, 1972. 266 pp.

A presentation of the psychological concepts of human behavior most relevant to the solution of management problems. Leavitt emphasizes the complexity of human behavior and the need for an understanding of basic behavioral processes. These processes are examined in sections dealing with the behavior of individuals, pairs, and small and large groups.

The effects of frustration, conflict, problem solving, values, and attitudes on individual behavior are discussed in a chapter on managerial decision making. A section on two-person relationships describes four methods of influencing behavior: authority, coercion, manipulation, and motivation. The author advocates an "alcoholics anonymous approach" as the best way to influence behavior. In this approach the person for whom behavioral modification is desired accepts the responsibility for changing himself.

The third section includes such topics as intergroup conflict and problem solving, communications networks, and individual conformity to group pressure. In the last section the special problems of large groups are placed in a systems framework composed of the dynamic, interrelated patterns of activity in the organizational elements of structure, technology, people, and tasks. Each organizational element is treated individually, in relation to the other elements and in relation to its societal environment.

Leavitt concludes that the major organizational problems

of the 1970's will be found in the latter category, as the organization tries to relate to its environment in response to the pressures of the times.

Likert, Rensis. *The Human Organization: Its Management and Value*. New York: McGraw-Hill Book Company, 1967. 258 pp.

This book, an extension of Likert's previous work, *New Patterns of Management*, emphasizes the importance of quantitative research as the foundation for a "science-based" system of management.

According to Likert, the best system of management will have more than a dozen characteristics, including complete confidence and trust between superiors and subordinates; participation by subordinates in setting goals, making decisions, and generating new ideas; extensive communication with a high degree of accuracy and acceptance; the identity of formal and informal organizations; and the process of relating decision-making groups.

A questionnaire is presented from which the management systems of departments and divisions can be evaluated. Some managerial practices and systems are assessed on a scale labeled "authoritarian-exploitative" at one extreme and "science-based" at the other.

In reviewing the research experience, Likert identifies three categories of variables: causal variables (the manager's plan of operation, high performance goals, technical competence, the "science-based" system of management); intervening variables (including group loyalty, cooperation, technical assistance to peers); and end-results variables (sales volume, sales costs, quality, earnings, and so on). Likert criticizes the tendency to measure the end-result variables, which are after-the-fact data. Periodic measurement of the causal and intervening variables can supply before-the-fact data, which would produce sounder plans, more effective programs, and less emergency action. He emphasizes the importance of explicitly measuring the human resources of the organization and estimating their economic value.

Mailick, Sidney, and Edward H. Van Ness, eds. *Concepts and Issues in Administrative Behavior.* Englewood Cliffs, N.J., Prentice-Hall, Inc., 1962. 202 pp.

This collection of articles about administrative behavior deals specifically with decision making, administrative organization, authority, communication, and human relations. The selection of articles demonstrates the various approaches taken by leading authors (William R. Dill, Herbert A. Simon, and Robert Presthus) in the field of administrative behavior.

Nord, Walter R., ed. *Concepts and Controversy in Organizational Behavior.* Pacific Palisades, Calif.: Goodyear Publishing Company, 1972. 600 pp. (paperback).

A collection of readings dealing with the management of human resources. Controversy is the guiding theme of the work; it explores the complex body of sociological and psychological knowledge and research concerning human behavior in organizations. A major conclusion is that an eclectic approach is best for understanding and managing human beings within the organizational milieu.

Part I focuses on individual behavior with regard to such concepts as basic human nature, perception, motivation, personality, and culture. The selections in Part II are oriented toward a systems approach for understanding formal organizations and their human problems. The third section of the book presents basic social-psychological issues in the study of organizational behavior, including communication, attitudes, group behavior, and leadership. The final section deals with the attempt to integrate behavioral science into the management of organizations. Helpful introductions are provided by the editor for each chapter and section.

Among the authors are Marshall McLuhan, Douglas Mc-Gregor, Abraham H. Maslow, Frederich Herzberg, B. F. Skinner, Peter Homans, Warren G. Bennis, and Chris Argyris.

Rush, Harold M. F. *Behavioral Science: Concepts and Management Application.* Report No. 216. New York, National Industrial Conference Board, Inc., 1969. 178 pp.

This comprehensive report applies the principles and findings of behavioral science to the management of the business organization. Five influential management theories are summarized: Douglas McGregor's "Theory X and Theory Y" on the manager's pessimistic or optimistic view of the nature of man in relation to his work; Abraham H. Maslow's "hierarchy of needs" (physiological, safety, belongingness and love, esteem, and self-actualization needs), and his concomitant theory that man is no longer motivated by a need which has been satisfied; Frederich Herzberg's concepts of job "satisfiers" and "dissatisfiers," along with his significant finding that "the opposite of satisfaction on the job is not dissatisfaction—instead, it is no satisfaction" and vice versa; Chris Argyris' concern with integrating the individual and the organization, job enlargement, and his "mix model" of organizational variables which indicate the health or sickness of an organization; and Rensis Likert's emphasis on the group-type organization and the member as a "linking pin" and connector of two groups, his four systems of management styles and the "Likert-type scale" for social research.

Three applications of the investigations of behavioral science are examined—sensitivity training, an organizational device known as the "managerial grid," and the Menninger Foundation Seminars for the training of industrial executives. The book concludes with a general survey and analysis of company use of behavioral science research for on-the-job situations. Ten case studies of various firms' applications of behavioral science are presented.

Schein, Edgar H. *Organizational Psychology*. 2d ed. Englewood Cliffs, N.J., Prentice-Hall, Inc., 1970. 138 pp.

Using a systems viewpoint, Schein discusses human problems and issues in organizations. Beginning with an individual orientation, he considers the recruitment, selection, training, and allocation of employees. He treats these topics as interrelated and inseparably tied to the social system of the total organization. Then moving to a group-and-system orientation, he discusses the problems of authority in the management process; managing groups and intergroup relationships; monitoring and controlling the interface between the internal organization and the external environment; and maintaining organizational effectiveness through a program of organizational development.

The process of maintaining a dynamic and effective organization in the face of internal and external environmental change is called the "adaptive-coping cycle." Consideration of this cycle points to areas of difficulty for management and provides a procedural framework for responding effectively to problem areas.

Townsend, Robert. *Up the Organization*. New York, Alfred A. Knopf, Inc., 1970. 202 pp.

Although Townsend writes about organizations in a witty and amusing way, he very seriously wishes to point out the absurdities of large organizations and shows little respect for the conventional thought behind organizational theory and behavior. He diagnoses boredom as a common illness peculiar to organizations, attacking everyone from mail boys and steno pools to presidents and vice-presidents. He objects to any kind of secrecy for marketing or planning new products because it implies either distrust or scandalous activities, and he thinks that the businessman should correct his mistakes openly. Firing is a lost art, he says, and though it is not an enjoyable experience, it must be done when a person is costing the company money.

The brief chapters include his thoughts on directors as puppets of the chief executive, suggestions for shorter and fewer meetings (remove all comfortable chairs and make participants stand), and a belief in private profit earned honestly. Townsend disapproves of such privileges as executive washrooms, dining rooms, chauffeurs, and paid expenses for the executive's family. This clever book pinpoints some significant but often unmentioned absurdities of organizational behavior.

C. Organization Change and Development

Argyris, Chris. *Integrating the Individual and the Organization*. New York, John Wiley and Sons, 1964. 330 pp.

It is Argyris' belief that certain factors implicit in traditional organization theory and practice lead to unintended, negative consequences for both the individual and the organization. In this book he develops a guide for redesigning organizations that includes research data to support the theory and a conceptual framework for testing the effectiveness of the proposed changes.

Central to Argyris' theory is the concept of psychological energy—the potential emotional energy each individual brings to an organization. Argyris argues that traditional organizations encourage defensive behavior that does not help the organization achieve its objectives. Defensive behavior becomes an end in itself, and the psychological energy that the individual could be using to further both his personal needs for self-development and the organization's goals is consumed in maintaining nonproductive internal systems.

To integrate the individual and the organization, the organization must be redesigned to decrease defensive activities—thereby freeing psychological energy—and to increase the opportunity for individuals to experience psychological success. In building this theory, Argyris also discusses specific areas of concern for managers: staffing, managerial control, rewards, hiring, evaluating, and firing.

Bennis, Warren G. *Organization Development: Its Nature, Origins, and Prospects*. Reading, Mass., Addison-Wesley Publishing Company Inc., 1969. 88 pp. Schein, Edgar H. *Process Consultation: Its Role in Organization Development*. Reading, Mass., Addison-Wesley Publishing Company Inc., 1969. 148 pp.

Only two of the six-volume Addison-Wesley series on organization development are listed here—the Bennis book because it gives the broadest perspective of the field of organization development (OD), and Schein's work because it describes an actual intervention and the behavioral-science theory behind the intervention strategy.

Bennis outlines what OD is and the conditions that created the need for it. Two excellent chapters in a question-and-answer format follow, one dealing with questions from professionals and the other with questions from managers about the OD process. After offering three examples of sensitivity-group failures in OD interventions, Bennis concludes with a discussion of other issues avoided by OD practitioners, particularly the issue of power in the politics of change.

Schein describes OD from his perspective as a process consultant. He discusses the important processes in an intervention: communication, problem solving, functional roles in groups, group problem solving and decision making, norms, leadership, authority, and the intergroup process. The stages of the actual intervention are outlined, including establishing contact and defining the consulting relationships, gathering data, and the techniques of the intervention, evaluation, and disengagement. The Bennis and Schein volumes provide a good general introduction to the theory and application of organization development.

Bennis, Warren G., Kenneth D. Benne, and Robert Chin, eds. *The Planning of Change: Readings in the Applied Behavioral Sciences*. 2d ed. New York, Holt, Rinehart and Winston, Inc., 1969. 628 pp.

This collection of readings concerns the application of systematic knowledge to human affairs for the purpose of planning intelligent action and change. It was written with the problems of professional practitioners in mind. Planned change is defined as a conscious effort to improve a system through the use of scientific knowledge. The book offers current ideas about differing aspects of the change process and introduces them with critical and theoretical commentary. The readings are organized around four major areas: (1) the historical roots of planned change, including the goals, values, and role of the social sciences, (2) conceptual tools for the change-agent with models of social systems and change, (3) models and dynamics of the influence process, and (4) the function, programs, and technologies of the planned-change process.

Blake, Robert R., and Jane S. Mouton. *Corporate Excellence Through Grid Organization Development.* Houston, Gulf Publishing Company, 1968. 374 pp.

Based on the grid which Blake and Mouton first described in *The Managerial Grid* (1964), this book is a systems approach to the achievement of corporate excellence. As such, it applies not to the individual but to the corporate entity. An excellent corporation strives to upgrade the sophistication of the technological aspects of marketing, production, research, and development, while increasing the competence of its managers and employees. Its aim is to ensure that its members commit themselves in an enthusiastic way to the accomplishment of corporate goals. Corporate excellence can be attained by the systematic and progressive administration of six major phases of grid organization development, which seek to improve corporate communication and planning and were developed by combining the results of research in business logic, management science, and behavioral science. The first three sections—"Grid Seminar," "Teamwork Development," and "Intergroup Development,"—deal with problems of communication and provide for development of the individual in his relationship to others. The next two—"Developing an Ideal Strategic Model" and "Planning and Implementation"—deal with problems of planning. The last section—"Systematic Critique"—evaluates the total effort and provides a basis for planning the next steps of development. The authors are concerned with teamwork, candor, conflict, and motivation. They present evidence of the applicability of their theory.

Fordyce, Jack, and Raymond Weil. *Managing with People: A Manager's Handbook of Organization Development Methods*. Reading, Mass., Addison-Wesley Publishing Company Inc., 1971. 192 pp.

This book illustrates some of the basic tools employed in organization development (OD) programs. The emphasis is on OD as a way of managing change and as a discipline for directing human energy toward specific goals. The authors view the methodology of OD as working jointly with those persons affected by the change. They consider the wants and needs of the individual to be essential inputs to the goal-setting process of the group.

The major section of the book discusses the use of meetings to bring about change and the ways to improve the quality of these meetings; the basic methods for collecting information about the current conditions within an organization; and methods for improving the quality of relationships among members of an organization through direct and open communication. The role and qualifications of the OD consultant are also discussed briefly, and four case studies are presented illustrating the process of change in the context of OD.

Harris, Thomas A. *I'm O.K. You're O.K.: A Practical Guide to Transactional Analysis*. New York, Harper and Row, Publishers, Inc., 1967. 278 pp.

Harris defines transactional analysis (TA) as a tool for understanding basic human feelings and behavior. According to the author, interchanges between people (transactions) are strongly influenced by the recordings of their earliest experiences. Although these experiences are not subject to recall, they may be unconsciously replayed in the present.

Transactional analysis assumes the existence of three stages of personality in every person: Parent, Adult, and Child. Fragile boundaries exist among the three states, and all persons have different degrees of each. This results in four possible "life positions" in regard to oneself and others:

1. I'm not O.K.—You're O.K.
2. I'm not O.K.—You're not O.K.
3. I'm O.K.—You're not O.K.
4. I'm O.K.—You're O.K.

By the end of early childhood an individual has accepted one of the first three positions and it becomes the dominant influence on the rest of his life. However, good mental health is reflected by position 4 ("I'm O.K.—You're O.K.") in which the person learns to rely more on the Adult instead of the Parent or the Child. This position may be attained by bringing the individual to an awareness of the childhood dilemmas underlying the first three positions, thus enabling him to overcome negative attitudes. Harris shows how to accomplish this by applying TA to marriage, child rearing, adolescence, moral values, and international relations.

Kaufman, Herbert. *The Limits of Organizational Change.* University, Ala., University of Alabama Press, 1971. 124 pp.

Kaufman believes that there are factors inherent in the structure and interpersonal relationships of organizations that make planned change improbable and that flexibility is directly related to an organization's size and age rather than to any particular strategy for changing it. He argues that the older an organization is the more flexible it is and the longer it may be expected to survive and that larger organizations are typically more flexible and more tolerant of unconventional ideas and behavior.

The barriers to planned change in organizations are the personal, psychological needs of people for predictability in their tasks and personal relationships and the tunnel vision of specialists who tend to lose sight of broader organizational goals. Limited resources are the main systemic obstacles to organizational change. Once an investment is made in new technology, new equipment, or other "sunk" costs, the committed resource tends to limit the latitude of the organization to change.

But organizations do change, and Kaufman characterizes

the change as either involuntary (personnel turnover) or voluntary (when an organization uses management experts, reorganizes itself, or actively recruits creative people and ideas). Yet new strategies for organizational change are self-limiting. Organizations like predictability: each change tends to limit further change, and the new orthodoxies tend to become as restrictive as the ones they replace.

Lippitt, Gordon L. *Organization Renewal: Achieving Viability in a Changing World.* New York, Appleton-Century-Crofts, 1969. 322 pp.

This book is a consideration of organization systems (both theory and research) that have been successfully tested by Lippitt's own work with organizational renewal in government, education, industry, and voluntary organizations. Lippitt sees organizational renewal as the process of confronting situations realistically so that problems are solved in a way that produces growth in individuals, groups, and the organization, as well as maturity in organizational problem solving.

He develops the conditions, skills, and activities necessary to produce organizational renewal from his own conceptual model of organizations. He presents theories about how organizations grow and function; systems of authority, communication, and power; and theories of leadership and motivation. Lippitt believes that the key element in organizational renewal is the effective functioning of people at work and that the evaluation of the renewal process must include determining its effects on the individual involved, as well as assessing the effectiveness of the change in the organizational setting. Annotated bibliographies follow each chapter.

Myers, M. Scott. *Every Employee a Manager: More Meaningful Work Through Job Enrichment.* New York, McGraw-Hill Book Company, 1970. 234 pp.

49

This book examines the strategies and techniques used in an extensive job-enrichment program at Texas Instruments, Inc., and provides practical guidance on how theory can be translated into management styles and systems by making the best use of available talent and energy.

Myers integrates the behavioral theories behind human relations, management by objectives, and the systems-planning approach to create a strategy for job enrichment. In general, Myers characterizes job enrichment as increasing the responsibility, sense of achievement, recognition, and growth of the individual in his job. Increasing the participation of the employee in control and planning functions necessarily closes the gap between labor and management, and Myers offers guidance on modifying the traditional role of the supervisor to allow employees to manage their own work. Attention is given to redefining the traditional functions of personnel and their place in job enrichment.

"Organization Development: An Overview," *Journal of Contemporary Business*, Summer, 1972. Seattle, University of Washington. 74 pp.

Several of the founding fathers of organization development—scholars and practitioners with national reputations—take a historical and critical look at OD in this special issue of the *Journal of Contemporary Business*. Broad coverage of problem areas in the field makes it a useful volume for both the scholar and the practicing manager.

Blake and Mouton discuss the theories of behavioral science that underlie OD, particularly those that support their own GRID organization development program. Richard Beckhard illustrates ways of bridging the gap between team leaders, who are interested in task and problem solving, and the OD consultant, who is often more interested in improving the workings and the interrelationships of team members.

Jack R. Gibb sees effective team building as a critical issue. Using his TORI method, Gibb presents ideas for managers attempting team building without consultants. David Bowers and Jerome Franklin, of the Institute for Social Research, believe that OD must demonstrate that it can improve the quantity, productivity, and quality of work. To aid in this demonstration, they recommend regular surveys of human resources to help in organizational change.

W. Warner Burke says that OD has rarely been used in designing new organizations but is used mostly in "putting out the fires" of bad interpersonal relationships. He says that OD practitioners must develop a better understanding of power dynamics if they are to move from organizational adaptation to actual organization development.

Reddin, W. J. *Managerial Effectiveness*. New York, McGraw-Hill Book Company, 1970. 352 pp.

The purpose of this book is to make the manager and his organization more effective by providing practical advice and a framework for action. The framework Reddin presents is his "3-D Theory of Managerial Effectiveness," which strives to develop three skills: diagnostic skill—the ability to read or evaluate a situation; style flexibility—the ability to change managerial styles to match different work situations; and situational management—the ability to change the work situation to match managerial style.

Reddin describes four basic managerial styles—integrated, related, dedicated, and separated—in terms of the degree of a manager's orientation toward relationships with other employees and the task at hand. Each style has a more or less appropriate side to it, providing a "3-D effect."

Five situational elements that affect managerial effectiveness are discussed: technology, subordinates, co-workers, superiors, and the organization. The author shows the manager how to appraise the demands and effects of these elements and concludes with practical advice on becoming a more effective manager and developing organizational effectiveness by applying the 3-D program.

Schmuck, Richard A., and Philip J. Runkel. *Handbook of Organization Development In Schools*. Eugene, Oreg., Center for the Advanced Study of Educational Administration, University of Oregon, 1972. 436 pp.

This comprehensive guide for facilitating human interaction in schools can be used profitably by specialists in any organization. The book includes an introduction to organizational development theory and technology and suggestions for setting up and evaluating training sessions. It deals chiefly with specific group functions within organizations and the methods and rationales for improving them: clarifying communications, establishing goals, uncovering and working with conflict, improving meetings, solving problems, and making decisions.

Coverage of each function includes theory and effectiveness criteria, testing instruments for assessing present and ideal conditions, a wide variety of exercises to stimulate movement toward the ideal state, follow-up procedures for using the new techniques in day-to-day work, and short readings that relate the methods and techniques to the larger body of literature.

III. THE ADMINISTRATIVE PROCESS

THE administrative process consists of all functions performed by management to achieve organizational goals. Thus planning and budgeting are part of the administrative process because they are actually performed by managers in reaching organizational objectives. Most enumerations of management functions tend to be arbitrary and reflect differences in emphasis rather than content. Henri Fayol, for example, stressed four basic functions: planning, organizing, commanding, and controlling. Luther Gulick identified seven functions: planning, organizing, staffing, directing, coordinating, reporting, and budgeting (POSDCORB). Others have focused on the decision-making aspect of management or on the importance of communication and control in organizations. In order to see management in a proper perspective, all administrative functions must receive adequate consideration. In this section is cited literature dealing with the important functions of decision making, planning, budgeting, leadership, motivation, communication, control, and evaluation. Works concerned with other functions of management, such as organizing and staffing, are found in Parts II and IV. It is important to realize that management functions are interrelated processes within the over-all task of management and that functional distinctions are made for analytical purposes only. They should never be interpreted as completely separate activities.

Decision making is at the heart of all managerial action. All of us make personal decisions affecting our own behavior, but a manager also makes organizational decisions that directly influence the behavior of others. A large part of his job involves making decisions, either as an individual or with the help of other individuals involved with one or several aspects of the decision-making process. As a decision maker the manager must translate organizational problems, opportunities, or disputes into specific organizational goals to be achieved; evaluate the consequences of alternative strategies; and implement the selected strategy. Books dealing with the nature of decision making and judgment have been included, as well as publications dealing with computers, operations research, and simulation and gaming.

Planning is a basic function for all managers at all levels in the organization. It involves setting goals and comparing alternative courses of action in terms of their relative cost and benefits and responsible choices to be made among them. All management functions are carried out to attain goals according to plans. Planning does not take place in a vacuum but takes into consideration the environment in which plans are supposed to be executed. Budgeting is simply planning for a given future period in quantitative terms. While the quantitative measures of a budget can be expressed in either monetary or nonmonetary terms, most budgets are expressed in monetary units. In the section dealing with planning and budgeting, most of the books are concerned with planning and budgeting in the public sector. Several of the works focus on the Planning-Programming-Budgeting System (PPBS), which combines program budgeting with systems analysis.

Highly regarded among managerial qualities is the ability

to lead effectively. Earlier leadership studies concentrated on analyzing personal leadership traits, while more recent research has centered on behavior patterns of leaders in various situations. In the management process leadership normally involves developing a work environment that is motivating. The better a manager understands what motivation is and how his subordinates are motivated the more effective he is likely to be as a leader. The books included in the section on leadership and motivation contain the theories of leadership and motivation most relevant to today's manager.

Communication plays a vital role in management. Most of a manager's work is done by communication. The scope of communication is extremely broad; it ranges from information theory to behaviorally oriented interpersonal communication. Even though many academic disciplines have studied communication, it has remained one of the biggest problems facing modern management. Effective communication is a basic prerequisite for effective organizational control. Control is the managerial function concerned with how well organizational objectives are being accomplished. Organizational control involves setting performance standards, evaluating performance, and taking corrective action. The common budget and PPBS are widely used control techniques. Several books listed in other sections are also relevant to the communication and control functions, such as those works on information systems, planning and budgeting, and evaluation.

Evaluation is basic to planning and control. In its complete form evaluation consists of stating objectives, identifying alternative ways to accomplish these objectives, choosing criteria for judgment, and analyzing outcome. The result of an evaluation may be used to select plans or programs, modify them while they are in progress, and determine how effectively an organization has achieved its objectives. This section includes works on evaluation research, managing social program evaluation, and cost-benefit analysis.

A. Decision Making

Barton, Richard F. *A Primer on Simulation and Gaming.* Englewood Cliffs, N.J., Prentice-Hall, Inc., 1970. 240 pp.

Barton provides a step-by-step introduction to simulation and gaming for members of the administrative professions and the behavioral sciences. "Real" object systems, the means by which these systems may be simulated, and four techniques for simulating the resulting models are illustrated. The four techniques are analysis, man-model simulation, man-computer simulation, and all-computer simulation. The differences between simulation and analysis are emphasized, and Barton argues strongly for the use of simulation only when analysis is difficult or impossible.

Three major simulation languages (DYNAMO, SIM-SCRIPT, and GPSS) are discussed, as well as flow diagrams and checklists for implementing various simulation programs and the nature and utilization of Monte Carlo techniques. Barton also considers the social aspects of obtaining service from computer personnel and gives practical advice for different types of computer applications and effective participation in the use of computer facilities. The primer concludes with a survey of teaching and research applications of simulation and gaming techniques in many fields.

Bocchino, William A. *Management Information Systems.* Englewood Cliffs, N.J., Prentice-Hall, Inc., 1972. 404 pp.

The objective of a management information system (MIS) is to provide accurate, timely, and meaningful information to decision makers. Bocchino discusses the tools and techniques available to develop an MIS and to analyze existing information flows in the organization. His presentation is pragmatic, stressing practical techniques of systems analysis and design.

He details in understandable terms work simplification, linear programming, and systems analysis and control techniques. He provides a comprehensive ten-step framework for an MIS study which can serve as a guideline for the systems analyst.

Brinkers, Henry S. *Decision Making: Creativity, Judgment, and Systems*. Columbus, Ohio State University Press, 1972. 276 pp.

This collection of essays develops in depth some important aspects of decision making. Six closely related conditions underlie the interdisciplinary approach of this work: (1) an increase in the complexity of "real-world" processes, (2) a shift of interest from quantity to quality as a measure of achievement, (3) a shift of interest from technological problems toward vastly more complex social problems and the nature of complex systems in general, (4) the increasing abandonment of the fragmentary ways of viewing the real world and the embracing of integrative views, (5) the general availability of low-cost, high-capacity information-processing technology, and (6) the evolution of a large body of scientific knowledge, drawn from research within several disciplines, which can express in precise terms the many relationships that can occur among large numbers of variables.

The general areas covered by these essays include the nature of decision making and its strategies, the contributions of various disciplines to the development of decision aids, the role of human creativity and judgment in decision making, and the implications and prospects for the future use of decision aids within academic and professional environments.

Brown, Ray E. *Judgment in Administration*. New York, McGraw-Hill Book Company, 1966. 226 pp.

Brown believes that administration is an art that can be

learned. In his view, judgment is central in administration: "Judgment is a composite process that brings into play the totality of an individual's traits and characteristics and represents a configuration of these traits, rather than the simple sum of them." His central thesis is that good judgment is natural to the administrative process, while poor judgment interferes with it. Brown writes about this aspect of administration from his own experience, as well as from observations of the performance of many administrators, and directs his attention to the causes of poor judgment in the administrative process.

The author categorizes these contributory factors in nine broad groups: stress, fear of defeat, feelings, continuous success, overconfidence in one's best skills, lack of professional attitude, inability to adapt, disproportionate attention to administrative activities, and overaddiction to numerical data. In discussing these factors, devoting a chapter to each, Brown is more concerned with those that cause good judgment to fail (and result in poor judgment) than with those that aid good judgment.

Design for Decision Making. Eighth Annual Review. Ottawa, Economic Council of Canada, 1971. 250 pp.

This examination of the major aspects of governmental decision-making processes in Canada is applicable to public decision making in the United States. The authors stress the need for a systematic and progressive approach to policy making and a wider dissemination of knowledge and information about policy issues to the general public.

After viewing the increasing role of government in Canadian society and a brief survey of some new approaches to decision making, the council traces the evolution of systematic analysis in the United States and Canada and discusses its use in answering broad policy questions. A framework for decision making is presented, and within this framework the main programs of federal manpower policy and certain facets of the formal educational systems in Canada are explored.

The council recommends the use of two statistical measures to improve the public decision-making process: (1) goal output indicators, to measure outputs of health, education, and public safety systems; and (2) goal distribution indicators, to show how the total output indicators are distributed among regions, income groups, ethnic groups, and so on. These indicators would provide a continuous monitoring system to ensure appropriate and timely action before problems reach crisis dimensions.

Elbing, Alvar O. *Behavioral Decisions in Organizations*. Glenview, Ill., Scott, Foresman and Company, 1970. 880 pp.

The purpose of this book is to help the manager develop effectiveness in making decisions in human systems. Accordingly, the author examines that process of decision making which is effective in the human dimension of organizational management and identifies several behavioral-science concepts necessary to a fundamental understanding of organizational behavior.

The book is divided into four sections. The first discusses the systematic approach to decision making in the human domain. The second presents a five-state decision-making model: (1) identifying a disequilibrium, (2) diagnosing the situation, (3) stating the problem, (4) selecting a course of action, and (5) implementing the selected solution. The third section furnishes basic readings in the area of human behavior directly relevant to the decision-making process. These readings present fundamental concepts for the study of the individual, two-person interaction, small groups and intergroup behavior, and the environment of the total organization as a social system. The final section discusses the value dimension inherent in all decision making.

Lyden, Fremont J., George A. Shipman, and Morton Kroll, eds. *Policies, Decisions and Organization*. New York, Appleton-Century-Crofts, 1969. 388 pp.

This collection of articles deals with research findings and analytic tools designed to stimulate studies in the area of decision making within governmental organizations. The authors develop an analytic framework for studying the decision-making process. They identify four kinds of decisions relevant to the four major phases in the organizational life cycle: (1) decisions involving the creation and maintenance of the organization; (2) decisions making operational the purpose of the organization; (3) decisions about organizing resources to accomplish objectives; (4) decisions determining whether the organization's objectives have been accomplished.

The first five sections of the book contain articles relevant to the organizational life cycle. Part Six is concerned with decision making as a process and with analytic constructs for studying particular aspects of the process. The last section contains two case studies of decision making in operation.

Marvin, Philip. *Developing Decisions for Action.* Homewood, Ill., Dow Jones-Irwin, Inc., 1971. 216 pp.

The ability to make effective decisions is a prerequisite for effective performance. Marvin believes that in order to develop decision-making skills it is necessary to go beyond a willingness to accommodate to change and become action-oriented. Action-oriented individuals are synoptic, dissatisfied with the way things are, sensitive to situations, catalytic, opportunistic, skill-directed, innovative, forward-thinking, resourceful, evaluative, expedient, and courageous. These twelve characteristics are common to effective decision makers and provide a frame of reference for those who want to increase their own decision-making effectiveness. The book offers the following rules for making good decisions: (1) make decisions that initiate and control action to do things identified as worthwhile, (2) make as few decisions as possible—only those for which guidelines cannot be formulated for others to use, (3) learn to spot decision-making situations that result in decisions that miss the mark, (4) analyze oneself in comparison to those who make effective decisions, (5) learn to understand the decision-making process, (6) compromise, (7) document one's decisions, (8) maintain a continuing awareness of the dimensions of one's decisions, (9) recognize artifices executives use to "save face," (10) enlarge the scope of one's goal-setting skills, (11) ask the right question of the right people, at the right time, about the right things, in the right detail, (12) learn to listen, (13) take the time to develop selling strategies that turn ideas into action, (14) conduct periodic audits of one's decision-making responsibilities, (15) learn to target decisions, and (16) be action-oriented.

Miller, David W., and Martin K. Starr. *Executive Decisions and Operations Research*. Englewood Cliffs, N.J., Prentice-Hall, Inc., 1969. 608 pp.

The authors examine executive decision problems in the framework of decision-theory formulation. They explain the use of a wide range of operations-research tools for problem solving, discuss the relationship of the decision-making process and operations research, and present an analysis of various problem situations faced by management. The techniques of decision-making theory and operations research are treated in such a manner that the reader need not have extensive training in mathematics to comprehend the material.

Odiorne, George S. *Management Decisions by Objectives.* Englewood Cliffs, N.J., Prentice-Hall, Inc., 1969. 252 pp.

The aim of this book is to improve the decision-making ability of the practicing manager. Because Odiorne believes it is impossible to develop a general theory of decision making, he synthesizes behavioral, mathematical, empirical, and intuitive methods into a practical approach.

The author describes the important steps of decision making as (1) defining the objective in such terms that progress toward its solution can be measured, (2) gathering the facts, (3) determining alternative courses of action and selecting the best one for achieving the objective, (4) implementing the decision, and (5) using feedback for controlling the effects of the decision. Odiorne stresses the importance of making a commitment to solve the problem and using a systematic method for making decisions. The problem is identified as the difference between the situation as it presently exists and what one would like for it to be.

A section entitled "Decision Making on the Run" is concerned with what to do when there is no time for the use of systematic logic in making a decision. The author cautions against overuse of the logic of system at the expense of the logic of practice. The final part of the book summarizes, with illustrations, tools for decision making. Nontechnical explanations of probability theory, sampling, statistical methods, and operations-research tools are presented.

Raser, John R. *Simulation and Society: An Exploration of Scientific Gaming*. Boston, Allyn and Bacon, 1969. 180 pp.

Raser presents an introduction to simulation and gaming, an important new research and teaching tool in the social sciences. He does not deal with the development and use of particular simulations; rather he explores what simulators are attempting to do and why. The first half of the book traces the philosophical, intellectual, historical, and epistemological roots of gaming. War games were the first simulations, and Raser examines the parallel development of simulation and gaming in such fields as management training, economic modeling, political and international-relations studies, sociology, psychology, and education. The second half of the book explores the utility of simulation in theory building and ways in which the techniques have been applied to training, teaching, and experimental research. The troublesome questions of validity of simulation and gaming are discussed, and, throughout, extensive examples and illustrations drawn from gaming literature give a good "feel" of the material. A bibliography organized by topics is included.

Simon, Herbert A. *Administrative Behavior: A Study of Decision-making Processes in Administrative Organization.* 2d ed. New York, The Free Press, 1957. 260 pp.

In this pioneering work the author lays the framework for a scientific theory of administrative organization by using decision making as a framework for analysis.

Simon points out the inadequacies of the "principles of administration"—those concerning specialization, unity of command, span of control, and so on—and condemns them as superficial, simplistic, and conflicting. The primary concern of administrative theory, he says, should be the rationality of decisions. Simon distinguishes between the roles of value judgments, which select final goals, and factual judgments, which implement the goals. He contrasts the psychological and logical bases of choice, concluding that human rationality operates within the limits of a psychological environment in which the organization influences individual behavior and decisions.

The author uses his framework to examine the major influences shaping decision making in the organizational environment: authority, efficiency, communications, and employee loyalty.

Stewart, William H., Jr. *Computers and Government.* Citizen Information Report No. 7. University, Ala., Bureau of Public Administration, University of Alabama, 1972. 54 pp. (paperback).

This survey of computer applications in federal, state, and local governments seeks to provide an acquaintance with the potential of data-processing equipment in the public sector. The view presented is that computers are inherently neither good nor evil—they serve or dominate humans in accordance with the wishes of the people who run them.

The author briefly describes the information-processing and decision-making uses of computers in four major governmental activities: financial administration (payrolls, governmental accounting, revenue collection), law enforcement (criminal information systems, project SEARCH, custom control), economic welfare (urban-information systems, job banks, weather prediction), and lawmaking (information retrieval on bills, drafting of legislation, scheduling).

Young, Stanley. *Management: A Decision-making Approach*. Belmont, Calif.: Dickenson Publishing Company, Inc., 1968. 146 pp. (paperback).

This is a collection of readings illustrating an interdisciplinary approach to decision making. The point of view of this small volume is that each discipline approaches decision making in terms of its own purpose and that each has something to offer to the managerial decision-making function. The first reading is a survey of contemporary decision-making analyses, with emphasis on economic decision making. Other readings review some of the contributions of mathematics, statistics, and physiology to decision making and deal with particular aspects of the decision process, such as creativity, rationality, uncertainty, and ethics. A final reading, which reviews the contribution of engineering to the decision process, discusses decision making within the context of total organization problem-solving systems. selected bibliography is included.

B. Planning and Budgeting

Anthony, Robert N. *Planning and Control Systems: A Framework for Analysis*. Boston, Division of Research, Graduate School of Business Administration, Harvard University, 1965. 180 pp.

The author discusses three main topics: strategic planning, management control, and operational control. He identifies strategic planning as policy formation, goal setting, and top management planning. Even though the term "management control" emphasizes control, planning is inherently associated with it. Management control here refers to that process by which a manager assures himself that resources are obtained and used effectively to achieve the objectives drawn in strategic planning. Three aspects of the process of management control are emphasized: (1) a manager himself is the key to achieving objectives, (2) the whole process operates within the context of the guidelines or objectives formulated in strategic planning, and (3) the criteria for judging actions are effectiveness and efficiency. Anthony also considers the topics of information handling and financial accounting.

Branch, Melville C. *Planning: Aspects and Applications*. New York: John Wiley and Sons, 1966. 334 pp.

Branch first explores the nature, types, and trends in institutionalized planning. From this general planning framework Branch considers four particular applications of planning: project planning, city planning, corporate planning, and military planning. These varied applications illustrate the wide applicability of the fundamental planning process. Branch shows how planning, in each application, responds to technological and socioeconomic developments. He reviews the comprehensive planning process by reviewing the fundamentals of coordinating planning and discussing such factors as quantification, people, objectives, and effect.

Emery, James C. *Organizational Planning and Control Systems: Theory and Technology.* New York, MacMillan Company, 1969. 166 pp.

As a synthesis of the various theoretical fields related to planning and control, this book develops a framework for viewing the general design and operation of a planning and control system. It is based on four basic premises: (1) in order to understand the planning process, one must understand the concept of systems, (2) formal planning requires information processing, (3) planning, like all other information processing, yields an output that has both a value and a cost, and (4) the theoretical construct underlying the process must be general enough to encompass many varieties of planning, concise enough to become a ready part of the designers' vocabulary of thought, and capable of explaining and justifying good planning practice. After considering the systems concept, Emery treats the organization as a system, outlines the role of the information system in the organization, and places planning in the proper context within the information system. In a discussion of the economics of information he develops a model to illustrate the value of information. The final chapter synthesizes organization theory, information science, and decision theory within the context of planning and control.

Haveman, Robert H., and Julius Margolis. *Public Expenditures and Policy Analysis.* Chicago, Markham Publishing Company, 1971. 596 pp.

The twenty-five papers included in this book are major contributions to the recent literature of the economics of public expenditure. They are arranged in five areas: (1) the economic basis of public expenditures, (2) institutional considerations in effective expenditure policy, (3) analytical problems in policy analysis, (4) the planning-programming-budgeting system (PPBS), and (5) policy analysis in federal programs.

The first set of papers analyzes the economic basis of public expenditures in terms of the economic functions of government, optimal division of resources between public and private enterprises, the need for and alternative approaches to collective action, and the income-redistribution effects of government expenditures. The second set of papers deals with such diverse institutional considerations as the roles of incentives and interest groups, the institutional constraints of the federal budget, and the limited knowledge of the distributive impact of public expenditures on society. The third section examines some of the basic problems encountered in estimating the costs and benefits of alternative public expenditure programs. The analytical problems examined include (1) the use of a social discount rate, (2) the appropriate treatment of risk and uncertainty, (3) the use of shadow prices, (4) the overstatement of real cost by monetary cost when unemployed resources are drawn into use by public expenditures, and (5) evaluation with multiple objectives. The fourth section evaluates the objectives of the PPBS, assesses its performance, and recommends changes in its structure and operation. The final section is concerned with economic analysis and program evaluation in selected functional areas of the federal budget such as PPBS in the Department of Defense, in the Department of Health, Education, and Welfare, and the Atomic Energy Commission.

Hinrichs, Harley H., and Graeme E. Taylor. *Program Budgeting and Benefit-Cost Analysis.* Pacific Palisades, Calif., Goodyear Publishing Company, 1969. 420 pp.

This introduction to public-expenditure analysis was the official text in the United States Civil Service Commission courses for federal middle-management trainees. The main section of the book contains a series of readings on program analysis, covering the role of analysis in program evaluation, the systems approach, the analysis of defense systems, the use of the input-output matrix in program budgeting, and the use of the discount rate. Additional papers deal with the rationale and theory underlying benefit-cost analysis, program structure, formulation of program objectives, development of effectiveness measures for judging goal attainment, and alternative measures for reporting program parameters. In the concluding section recommendations are made for future development of the planning-programming-budgeting system. Several cases are included to test and apply the theory underlying the analysis.

This book has been followed and complemented by the authors' *Systematic Analysis: A Primer on Benefit-Cost and Program Evaluation* (Pacific Palisades, Calif., Goodyear Publishing Company, 1972, 152 pp.). The authors survey the major categories of systematic analysis: objectives, constraints, externalities, the interest-rate problem, and risk and uncertainty. Four case studies and four completed analytical studies illustrate the different kinds of systematic analysis. An appendix presents some brief notes on planning, analysis, and evaluation.

Kahn, Alfred J. *Theory and Practice of Social Planning.* New York, Russell Sage Foundation, 1969. 348 pp.

This wide-ranging study of social planning in the United States—its process, history, and relationship to American values—touches on myriad aspects of social welfare programs, institutions, and services.

In developing a model for social planning action, Kahn emphasizes the complexity of the planning process and the many external considerations that are necessary. The planning process is seen as a "series of intersecting circles or spirals" rather than a linear procedure. He lists five stages: (1) preplanning or preliminary investigation, (2) definition of planning tasks or goals, (3) formulation of policy to be pursued, (4) program selection, and (5) feedback, measurement, and evaluation. The concepts of social planning, social service, values, social policy, community organization, imperative planning, incremental planning, task force planning and urban planning are defined and discussed.

A companion volume, *Studies in Social Policy and Planning*, (New York, Russell Sage Foundation, 1969. 326 pp.) is a series of case studies used to illustrate and elaborate the policy and planning framework presented in the work above. The studies embrace six fields of contemporary concern in social planning: the war on poverty, juvenile delinquency, income security, city planning, community psychiatry and local-level social service delivery. The works are useful for students and practitioners in the field of social services and anyone desiring a comprehensive overview of the social-planning process.

Kelleher, Grace J., ed. *The Challenge to Systems Analysis: Public Policy and Social Change*. New York, John Wiley and Sons, 1970. 150 pp.

This is a collection of introductory readings on the application of systems analysis to social problems. The first section briefly covers the history and development of operations research and systems analysis as management tools. The second and main section deals with the application of systems analysis in such areas as urban problems, highway safety, international communications, population control, computer-assisted instruction, and the world food problem. A concluding essay comments on the underlying structure of systems analysis as it developed and on its general application to the social sciences. The essays, written largely by individuals in public office and organizations directly involved with social problems on a day-to-day basis, offer a clear perspective of past, current, and future possibilities for effective uses of systems analysis.

Levin, Richard I., and Charles A. Kirkpatrick. *Quantitative Approaches to Management*. New York, McGraw-Hill Book Company, 1965. 366 pp.

The first eight chapters of this book deal with the Program Evaluation and Review Technique (PERT) and the last deals with the Critical Path Method (CPM). Knowledge and understanding of PERT is prerequisite to comprehending CPM. This work describes what PERT is and does and where it can be used by managers. The book provides a brief description of twenty-nine current project-planning and control techniques which have grown out of the original PERT and CPM techniques. A comprehensive bibliography on PERT and CPM is included.

Lyden, Fremont J., and Ernest G. Miller, eds. *Planning, Programming, and Budgeting: A Systems Approach to Management*. 2d ed. Chicago, Markham Publishing Company, 1972. 424 pp.

The first edition of this book, published in 1968, was a collection of articles that defined the planning-programming-budgeting (PPB) approach, what its limitations and deficiencies were, and how it related to other kinds of budgeting and to systems analysis in general. This second edition, a major departure from the earlier book, emphasizes the problems that confronted the various government agencies as they implemented PPB. Its aim is to help practitioners cope with such problems as how to develop the program structure and PPB budgeting format, what analytic methods to use when implementing PPB, and how to measure program impact. The book discusses the historical background of PPB, budgeting as a political process, the program planning and evaluation base of budgeting, the incorporation of program plans into the PPB budgeting format, the rationale underlying some of the major analytic techniques used in PPB, the implementation of PPB in government agencies, and the prospects of PPB in view of the various criticisms that it has received.

Merewitz, Leonard, and Stephen H. Sosnick. *The Budget's New Clothes: A Critique of Planning-Programming-Budgeting and Benefit-Cost Analysis.* Chicago, Markham Publishing Company, 1971. 318 pp.

A critical analysis of planning-programming-budgeting (PPB) and its subfield, benefit-cost analysis. The authors investigate five principle elements of PPB: program accounting, multiyear costing, detailed measurement and description of activities, zero-base budgeting, and benefit-cost analysis. Particular emphasis is placed on the last element, with considerations of who should perform a benefit-cost analysis, which criteria should be used, and the importance of externalities and constraints. The work includes case studies of benefit-cost analyses in two large public investments, the California Water Project and the supersonic transport (SST) program. Findings are that PPB had a minimal impact on decision making in these projects and that the criterion of efficiency was largely ignored.

The authors propose that PPB be used in choosing among alternative projects rather than deciding whether or not to undertake a particular project. The criterion of efficiency should be balanced with the program's equity and merit. Most importantly, PPB should be implemented only after giving careful thought to the potential benefits and costs of using the PPB process.

Schick, Allen. *Budget Innovation in the States.* Washington, D.C., Brookings Institution, 1971. 224 pp.

Schick examines and compares the two major state budgetary reform movements of the last two decades: performance budgeting in the 1950's and planning-programming-budgeting (PPB) in the 1960's. Performance budgeting is primarily concerned with efficient management of the activities of public agencies, and PPB has been primarily involved with program planning. An assessment of the two reform attempts leads the author to conclude that both run against the grain of budget traditions, such as incremental budgeting, which were established early in the twentieth century. They have faced common administrative difficulties in promoting budgetary change owing to an inability to overcome the earlier traditions. Despite all the publicity and excitement about PPB, it has not yet been implemented to any great degree in the states, and its progress has been minimal, its initial results disappointing, and its future directions uncertain. Nevertheless, the concepts and components of PPB will probably remain even if the technique itself fails, and it has led to improvement in the budget practices of some of the states. Schick concludes that although meaningful budget innovation is very difficult, it is still possible through implementation of better planning and more thorough program evaluation.

Schultze, Charles L., *et al. Setting National Priorities: the 1973 Budget*. Washington, D.C., Brookings Institution, 1972. 468 pp.

This book examines the basic assumptions that underlie the 1973 budget, the budget's present and future implications as a public policy-making instrument, and feasible alternatives to important budgetary strategies. This, the third volume of an annual series, highlights such policy areas as national defense, welfare, health insurance, child care, urban fiscal problems, elementary and secondary education, and the environment. The budget's importance in setting national priorities in these and other areas is emphasized, along with its role as an allocator of resources through expenditures and taxation.

Two major themes of the book are (1) the budgetary process must not only be concerned with how *much* to spend but also with how *best* to spend it in accordance with national objectives and (2) budgetary decisions have their greatest consequences not immediately but several years later. These two considerations, as well as the expectation that federal expenditures will continually surpass federal revenues, indicate the increasing need for better and longer-range budgetary planning, greater utilization of government incentives to aid in accomplishing national goals, and more federal program experimentation.

Wildavsky, Aaron. *The Politics of the Budgetary Process.* 2d ed. Boston, Little, Brown and Company, 1974. 272 pp.

This work analyzes federal budgeting as a political process founded on incrementalism. Wildavsky explains the budgetary process from the viewpoint of its participants (such as the Bureau of the Budget and the appropriations committees) and describes the strategies government agencies employ to maintain or increase their share of the federal pie. The major strategy is good agency politics, cultivating an active and effective clientele, imbuing other government officials with confidence in the agency, and exploiting the agency's opportunities.

After considering the politics of budgetary reform and appraising current budgetary practices and suggested alternatives, the author concludes that the traditional procedures work better than commonly believed and remain superior to any reform proposals made to date. This is primarily due to the complexity of the budgetary process. We know so little about how it really works that broad, intelligent, and meaningful reform is virtually impossible.

The second edition of this book includes two new chapters, one on program budgeting and one on restoring congressional control of the budget.

C. Leadership and Motivation

Argyris, Chris. *Executive Leadership: An Appraisal of a Manager in Action.* Hamden, Conn., Archon Books, 1967. 140 pp.

This report examines a specific leader and how his behavior affects the daily lives of his supervisors. Argyris first describes the distinguishing features of the executive as a leader by comparing the researcher's impressions of the executive's leadership with the executive's own impressions.

To describe the effects of this leader's behavior on his twenty supervisors, Argyris observed the supervisors to determine whether their behavior changed because of the leader's absence or presence; he then related the behavior of these supervisors to a leadership pattern. Problems faced by the supervisors in adapting to the leader are discussed.

Argyris examines the leader of today, summarizes the lessons to be learned, and makes recommendations to the reader for action. Details about research methods and problems encountered in the investigation are given in appendices.

Cribbin, James J. *Effective Managerial Leadership.* New York, American Management Association, 1972. 264 pp.

Cribbin's thesis is that there is no prescription or formula to ensure successful leadership; different kinds of leadership behavior are suited to different circumstances. To select the best leadership model for a given situation, four variables must be considered: the personality of the leader, the personality of the group, organizational factors, and the over-all work situation.

The author examines the macro factors, such as the surrounding culture, subcultures, ethos, and political structure, and the micro factors, managerial strategies, role concepts, and attitudes that influence leadership. He stresses that organizational reality is found not in official documents and organizational charts but in such variables as authority and power relationships, informal groups, and status systems. Useful suggestions are offered in many areas, including understanding subordinates and their needs, employee motivation, effective communications, development of subordinates to give them a sense of purpose, tensions and means of coping with them, business ethics and morality, and managerial leadership and change.

Fiedler, Fred E., and Martin M. Chemers. *Leadership and Effective Management.* Glenview, Ill., Scott, Foresman and Company, 1974. 166 pp.

The focus of this work is on the determinants of effective leadership within management.

A review of the literature shows that research findings on leadership have been rather inconclusive, particularly those concerned with the influence of leader behavior on employee performance and satisfaction and those attempting to identify and select effective leaders.

The authors cite evidence that group performance is contingent upon (1) the leader's motivation, which can be task-oriented or relationship-oriented, and (2) the favorableness of the situation, as determined by leader-follower relations, task structure, and positional power of the leader. Fiedler's "Contingency Model of Leadership Effectiveness" is presented, which shows that task-motivated people perform best if they have either a great deal of, or very little, control and influence over their situation and that relationship-motivated people perform better if their control and influence are moderately high. The authors feel that a lack of attention to motivation and situation accounts for the fact that most studies have shown that leadership training and experience do not contribute positively to management performance. As an alternative to formal leadership training the authors provide general guidelines for application of their contingency model to improve leadership effectiveness.

Herzberg, Frederick. *Work and the Nature of Man.* Cleveland, World Publishing Company, 1966. 204 pp.

This volume is a continuation of the author's study on work motivation. The main emphasis is on Herzberg's motivation-hygiene theory, which examines man's conflicting desires to avoid pain, on the one hand while seeking to discover, achieve, and progress on the other.

The motivation aspect of the theory (motivator needs) is concerned with such factors as responsibility, achievement, advancement, recognition, and the nature of work itself; the hygiene part (hygiene needs) deals with supervision, company policies and administration, working conditions, salary, and job security. The author extensively discusses motivator needs and promotion of the psychological growth of employees. He notes that current public administration in industry is inclined to fulfill man's hygiene needs and points out that this tendency may lead to the neglect of motivator needs. Herzberg recommends that organizational structures be designed so that there are two formal divisions of industrial relations, one concerned with hygiene needs, the other, with motivator needs.

Levinson, Harry. *The Great Jackass Fallacy.* Boston, Division of Research, Harvard Business School, 1973. 178 pp.

The "jackass fallacy" refers to the common assumption that rewards and punishments are what motivate people, evidenced by the carrot-and-stick approach, where the boss is a manipulator of his subordinate, the jackass. This fallacy is the major cause of management-labor difficulties and other organizational problems. Combined with the bureaucratic organizational structure, where those at the bottom of the hierarchy are dependent upon those at the top, it presents an imposing obstacle to organizational survival.

In this book, which synthesizes nine previously published articles, the author shows that the most powerful human motivators are not rewards and punishments but the individual's desire to attain his ego ideal—his ideal best self. This Levinson calls "psychological man." The concept of psychological man is employed to explain the roots of personal and organizational problems and to illustrate how these problems can be prevented or eliminated.

McGregor, Douglas. *The Human Side of Enterprise*. New York, McGraw-Hill Book Company, 1960. 246 pp.

Research findings in the behavioral sciences led McGregor to formulate a new theory of management (Theory Y) to replace traditional management theory, which he called Theory X. Theory X assumes that people inherently dislike work, shy away from responsibility, and consequently must be controlled in order to get work done. Under Theory X, therefore, management's job is to direct and control work, using firm authority. McGregor believes that these assumptions are inadequate (or inaccurate) for explaining human behavior in organizations. Using social science research, especially the "hierarchy of human needs" as formulated by Abraham H. Maslow, McGregor proposes a new theory of management that assumes that man wants to work, is self-directing and self-controlling, and accepts responsibility. Under such a theory the manager's job is, obviously, quite different: to create conditions that permit subordinates to achieve their own goals by directing their own efforts toward the success of the organization.

The book examines the implications of Theory Y for certain managerial activities, such as performance appraisal, wage and salary administration, line-staff relationships, participative management, and the dilemmas created by traditional ideas about management.

Raia, Anthony P. *Managing by Objectives*. Glenview, Ill., Scott, Foresman and Company, 1974. 200 pp.

This book provides a clear understanding of the fundamental concepts and tools required to design and implement an effective management by objectives (MBO) system. According to the author, there is no one best way to manage by objectives. Each program must be tailored to the needs and circumstances of a given organization.

Raia identifies the three main aspects of MBO: (1) it is a philosophy of management that reflects a proactive rather than a reactive way of managing, (2) it is a process of formulating concise objectives, developing realistic action plans for their attainment, systematically monitoring and measuring performance and achievement, and taking corrective actions necessary to achieve the planned results, and (3) it is a system of management designed to integrate the key managerial processes and activities in a logical and meaningful way.

The first two chapters in this book provide a conceptual overview of MBO. The following chapters discuss goals and objectives for the organization and its subunits, job objectives for the individual manager, action planning, motivation, performance appraisal, and key organizational relationships. The final chapter presents several case studies to illustrate how an MBO system might be installed.

An excellent annotated bibliography on MBO is included.

Smits, Stanley J. *Leadership Behavior of Supervisors in State Rehabilitation Agencies*. Atlanta, Georgia State University, 1971. 62 pp.

This research monograph explores the complex links between the leadership style of rehabilitation supervisors and the job satisfaction and productivity of rehabilitation counselors. Leadership style was assessed from the point of view of both the counselors and the supervisors with test instruments designed to measure leadership behavior, interpersonal problem-solving orientation, and work activities. The results indicated the importance of intervening organizational and individual variables in the supervisory leadership process. Counselors and supervisors tended to describe the supervisor's leadership behavior in a similar manner; counselors attached great importance to the quality of interpersonal relationships they had with their supervisors.

In terms of leadership behavior, rehabilitation supervisors predominantly perform evaluative activities, and their supervisory activities seem largely a function of the number of counselors whom they supervise. The supervisors' leadership styles were significantly related to their orientation toward interpersonal problem solving.

The monograph also reports a follow-up study on the ability of "The Job Satisfaction Inventory" to predict employment termination/retention (it could), and an oral and written communication experiment within a state rehabilitation agency (counselors received and retained less than supervisors).

Vroom, Victor H. *Work and Motivation.* New York, John Wiley and Sons, 1964. 332 pp.

Dealing primarily with the effects of motivation on work roles and the effects of work roles upon motivation, this book is concerned with choice of work role, job satisfaction, and performance.

The author reports that people work not only for economic gain but also to use and develop skills, gain social status, and contribute something useful to society. He summarizes research on occupational choice and finds that job selection is determined by individual preference influenced by estimates of probable attainment of occupational objectives. Research also indicates that job satisfaction results from high wages, good opportunities for promotion, considerate and participative supervisors, an opportunity for interaction with co-workers, varied work tasks, and a high degree of control over work methods and the pace of work. Vroom states that, in addition to these situational variables, job satisfaction is accounted for by individual personality differences. He determines that there is a negative relationship between job satisfaction and employee turnover and absences and no relationship between job satisfaction and job performance. In examining the effect of motivation upon work performance, Vroom finds that higher performance tends to result from higher wages, co-worker acceptance, promotion, the individual's need for achievement, performance feedback, and participative decision making.

D. Communication and Control

Foltz, Roy G. *Management by Communication*. Philadelphia, Chilton Book Company, 1973. 146 pp.

Since most of a manager's work is accomplished through communication and communication depends upon human behavior and not rules, the manager must be aware of his employees' basic desires to know, understand, and contribute to their jobs. Foltz emphasizes this theme throughout the book as he deals with the factors that create successful relationships within an organization. Primary consideration is given to problems of motivation, changing attitudes toward the work ethic, and the need for people who know how to listen. The author advises companies to audit their communication systems regularly and suggests ways to accomplish this by interviews and questionnaires.

Management by Communication is a treatise for developing well-rounded individuals, which should lead to the improved performance of the organization.

Gallagher, William J. *Report Writing for Management*. Reading, Mass., Addison-Wesley Publishing Company, 1969. 216 pp.

Designed for those who submit reports to management or those who must review or request reports, this book treats report writing as a creative exercise for the writer, the reviewer, and the user. The author views reports as the essence of management information and control systems and takes a systems approach to the interrelated tasks required in report writing. His step-by-step approach entails stating and defining the problem and the scope of the report, planning the research, collecting and analyzing information, forming conclusions, organizing the report, preparing the first draft, editing the draft, and publishing the report. A review of grammar is included, emphasizing conciseness, clarity, and accuracy in writing. Examples of good and bad writing are given to illustrate the author's points.

Haney, William V. *Communication and Organizational Behavior.* 3d ed. Homewood, Ill., Richard D. Irwin, Inc., 1973. 584 pp.

The focus of this book is on "miscommunication" patterns. Haney provides a brief overview of the influence of organizational climate on communication and the role of perceptions and motivations in communication. He then discusses typical communication problems that cause misunderstanding, confusion, and conflict. The causes of these problems are explored, as are means for reducing their occurrence. Many examples are provided to illustrate communication problems, a number of which are valuable in developing an understanding of miscommunication patterns. The final section of the book provides an extensive bibliography for the reader interested in selected communication topics.

Hayakawa, Samuel Ichiye. *Language in Thought and Action.* 2d ed. New York, Harcourt-Brace and World, Inc., 1964. 350 pp.

The author writes:

This book is devoted to the study of the relationships between language, thought, and behavior. . . . The basic assumption . . . [will be] that widespread . . . cooperation through the use of language is the fundamental mechanism of human survival. A parallel assumption will be that when the use of language results, as it so often does, in the creation or aggravation of disagreements or conflicts, there is something wrong with the speaker, the listener or both.

In the first half of his book Hayakawa explains "the functions of language," starting with an examination of the symbolic process. He makes careful distinctions among reports, inferences, and judgments. The fact that a reader or listener invests a word with meaning from the context in which it is set leads to a discussion of "extensional" and "intensional" meaning. Language has two tasks—making things happen and expressing feelings. The author provides three informative chapters on these uses.

In the second half of the book, entitled "Language and Thought," the author demonstrates that many of man's difficulties stem from his failure to see his world clearly and the disparities between what he sees and the statements he makes about those "sights." Language can "go wrong" in various ways. Elements contributing to confusion in perceptions are confusing words with things; confusing levels of abstraction; failing to distinguish a fact, an inference, and a judgment; believing in absolutes; making false identifications; using a two-value orientation; and believing in the power of words. Hayakawa examines, with great wit and skill, each of these difficulties.

Kaufman, Herbert. *Administrative Feedback: Monitoring Subordinates' Behavior*. Washington, D.C., Brookings Institution, 1973. 84 pp.

In this study of administrative feedback from subordinates to leaders in nine federal agencies, the author's contention is that there is an abundance of feedback available to leaders in various forms, giving them ample means to keep track of their subordinates' behavior. But much that happens at lower levels within the agencies is not detected by leadership, owing to negative motivation caused by such limitations as excessive cost, information overload, and leaders' unreceptiveness to unfavorable feedback. A strategy for improvement is offered: induce leaders to make better use of existing feedback by restructuring their incentives. Suggestions are to redefine leadership responsibility by holding leaders responsible for actions of their subordinates, increase extra-agency evaluation of subordinate behavior, and conduct interviews with the agency's clientele.

Keefe, William F. *Listen, Management! Creative Listening for Better Managing.* New York, McGraw-Hill Book Company, 1971. 200 pp.

Keefe believes that of the four communications skills—reading, writing, speaking, and listening—the ability to listen is the most important for managers. He defends listening as a neglected art that must be mastered for effective communications and good management.

The importance of creative listening is stressed. It requires an open and mature attitude toward other people and patience. It is necessary to listen not only to the words of the speaker but also to what lies behind the words—what the speaker actually means. The author reviews rules of good listening found in management literature and shows how they can be used to motivate employees, develop teamwork and morale, encourage creativity, ease organizational change, and eliminate emotional blocks and filters to effective communications. Many illustrations are given of the successful use of creative listening and of the disasters that can befall the manager who fails to listen to others.

Mockler, Robert J. *The Management Control Process.* New York, Appleton-Century-Crofts, 1972. 358 pp.

The main thesis of this book is that management control is an integrated scientific discipline; it encompasses all control activities within an organization and has its own set of principles and processes to direct the manager in dealing with business-control situations. Mockler points out the need for a unifying concept of control incorporating both modern and traditional viewpoints and the importance of establishing specific organizational groups responsible for coordinating all control activities within a company.

The author first shows how the management control process parallels the problem-solving—decision-making process. He then lists specific preparatory steps necessary for management control and discusses the key factors affecting control situations, such as environmental factors and economic and marketing forecasting. The uses of graphic and mathematical tools and information-processing systems are considered, as well as accounting and finance controls and operating and staff controls.

Two chapters study actual management-control situations: (1) an over-all corporate financial control system and (2) an operating-control network in the marketing area. The book concludes with a history of the theory and practice of management control.

Murphy, Herta A., and Charles E. Peck. *Effective Business Communications.* New York, McGraw-Hill Book Company, 1972. 784 pp.

A comprehensive guide to planning, organizing, and implementing effective business communications. The authors stress the importance of keeping the receiver in mind while writing letters, memos, and reports. Their aim is to help the writer compose messages that the receiver can easily understand and to which he will react favorably.

Murphy and Peck present basic writing principles and discuss, in depth, routine requests, good and bad news, persuasive requests, job applications, collections, and goodwill letters, and various kinds of reports. A chapter devoted to oral communications deals with speaking, listening, and interviewing. Appendices contain sections on the legal aspects of business communications, mechanics and style, suggestions for cutting correspondence costs, and symbols used in proofreading.

Sigband, Norman B. *Communication for Management.* Glenview, Ill., Scott, Foresman and Company, 1969. 762 pp.

Emphasizing the importance of communication in conducting a successful business, this book offers practical advice on how to communicate effectively.

The first section considers communication theories and processes and discusses communication as a tool of management control. The author considers the various kinds of organization media—pay-envelope inserts, orientation manuals, the grapevine. The second section covers techniques of business writing with emphasis on reports. Included are chapters on research, the process of writing, use of visual aids, and the job résumé. The third section is devoted to business letters; various examples are listed, and writing methods are surveyed. A collection of readings selected for relevance to the book's topics is included.

Illustrations of styles and forms are generously provided. Appendices present a guide to grammar and word usage, a guide to secondary resources, and examples of letter style and format.

Thayer, Lee. *Communication and Communication Systems*. Homewood, Ill., Richard D. Irwin, Inc., 1968. 376 pp.

This book is a general study of the communication process. It is the author's belief that the essence of being human is to "be-communicated-to" and "be-communicated-with." Rather than stressing communication methods and techniques, the author is concerned with how behavior and attitudes affect communication effectiveness.

Thayer discusses effective communication on the individual level, the group level, the organizational level, and the technological level. Communication effectiveness is determined by individual values, beliefs, and backgrounds, as well as the ability to comprehend the intended message. The author also discusses motivation, kinds of messages, communicative functions, and various communication problems.

Each chapter is followed by a bibliography, and two appendices are included: one on how to write and the other on managerial reports.

E. Evaluation

Barsby, Steve L. *Cost-Benefit Analysis and Manpower Programs*. Lexington, Mass., D. C. Heath and Company, 1972. 180 pp.

Barsby's book is a broad evaluation of the contributions of cost-benefit analysis in the manpower field. Following a brief discussion of the components of cost-benefit analysis and the various problems encountered in estimating costs and benefits, the author examines eighteen cost-benefit studies of manpower programs. The programs analyzed include vocational education in secondary and post-secondary schools, institutional out-of-school manpower programs, programs with an on-the-job-training component, vocational rehabilitation, Job Corps, and Work Experience and Training programs. Barsby emphasizes that the calculation of a benefit-cost ratio is a sterile exercise unless it is accompanied by a detailed analysis of labor-market experiences and the results obtained. Over all, the studies suggest that the benefits of manpower programs exceed costs and that vocational rehabilitation is the most efficient large-scale manpower program. The final chapter summarizes the results of the cost-benefit analyses and concludes that the greatest potential of this kind of evaluation lies in internal analysis of programs as opposed to a comparative analysis between programs. An extensive bibliography is included.

Caro, Francis G., ed. *Readings in Evaluation Research*. New York, Russell Sage Foundation, 1971. 418 pp.

This is a general survey of the field of evaluation research. The papers are arranged under the general areas of (1) the nature of program evaluation, (2) its role in social programs, (3) the organizational context of evaluation, and (4) methodological strategies for evaluation research. Specific topics—treated by such authorities on program evaluation as Edward Suchman, Carol Weiss, and Peter Rossi—include the need for evaluation, researcher-practitioner problems and relations, use of the scientific method in evaluation, utilization of control groups, and research design. A helpful overview of the field is provided by the editor. Case studies show how principles of evaluation research have been applied to specific program situations.

Dorfman, Robert, ed. *Measuring Benefits of Government Investments.* Washington, D.C., Brookings Institution, 1965. 430 pp.

The papers in this volume are concerned with the usefulness of benefit-cost analysis in evaluating government investment programs. An introductory paper briefly outlines the benefit-cost framework. Others discuss the use of benefit-cost analysis in the areas of research and development expenditures, outdoor-recreation projects, education programs, civil-aviation expenditures, highway investments, urban-renewal projects, and public health programs. Most of these papers are followed by at least two comments from practitioners in various governmental agencies, in some instances challenging the various theoretical aspects of the models employed in the analyses and in others conveying doubt that the most important social effects of government investment programs could ever be evaluated quantitatively.

Grigg, Charles M., Alphonse G. Holtman, and Patricia Y. Martin. *Vocational Rehabilitation for the Disadvantaged.* Lexington, Mass., D. C. Heath and Company, 1970. 276 pp.

This interdisciplinary study of fourteen research and demonstration projects, conducted under the sponsorship of state vocational-rehabilitation (VR) agencies, reports on two aspects of evaluation: (1) a process analysis of the VR program and (2) an evaluation of the rehabilitation process with regard to its benefits and costs.

In the first section the authors examine the selection process for entrance into the projects and the factors related to rehabilitation outcome. The factor related closest to project acceptance is identified as the number of evaluative services received by clients during referral; the single factor found to be most closely related to rehabilitation outcome is total services rendered during the rehabilitation program. The second section deals with some of the theoretical aspects of the economics of VR, and an economic model for evaluating VR expenditures is developed. A regression model is used to give the cost-benefit model empirical content. The authors emphasize that the high economic returns reported in this study do not take into account many other social and individual benefits and conclude that vocational rehabilitation programs are sound investments for the public and the individuals receiving services.

Hatry, Harry P., Richard E. Winnie, and Donald M. Fisk. *Practical Program Evaluation for State and Local Government Officials*. Washington, D.C., Urban Institute, 1973. 134 pp.

This practical guide on how to plan and conduct an evaluation identifies three major steps in the evaluation process: defining program objectives; developing means to measure progress toward the objectives, and identifying the program's target population. Comparative evaluation designs are discussed, along with various procedures for collecting evaluation data. Guidelines are presented for obtaining personnel to conduct the evaluation, funding the evaluation, and recognizing limitations of the evaluation process. Specific recommendations include (1) establishing federal evaluation of state and local government programs receiving federal funds, (2) providing explicitly for an evaluation component in federal demonstration and experimental programs, (3) developing better methods for disseminating evaluation results, and (4) providing more training for evaluation personnel. A case study and factual examples underline the authors' major points.

Mishan, E. J. *Economics for Social Decisions: Elements of Cost-Benefit Analysis.* New York, Praeger Publishers, Inc., 1973. 152 pp.

This book, a nonmathematical key to understanding the basic rationale and concepts of cost-benefit analysis, begins with a brief discussion of cost-benefit analysis as it relates to the Pareto improvement criterion. Then follows a concise treatment of some of the rudimentary concepts underlying the analysis, such as consumer surplus, rents, transfer payments, and shadow prices. Several chapters deal with the evaluation of spillover effects, including changes in the incidence of death, disablement, or disease as a result of project or program operation. One section is devoted to the presentation and comparison of the various criteria for judgment in cost-benefit analysis and includes a discussion of the discount rate. The final chapters develop some of the methods for dealing with future risk.

O'Toole, Richard, ed. *The Organization, Management, and Tactics of Social Research.* Cambridge, Mass., Schenkman Publishing Company, Inc., 1971. 312 pp.

This book of readings analyzes the organization, management, and tactics of social research; the research process and its results; and the effects of research on social programs. The major assumption is that a knowledge of methodology alone is not sufficient for conducting a successful research project. Various contingencies that may arise during and after the research process, such as lack of cooperation among persons involved with the research or unpopular findings, must be resolved. The selections in this work discuss such contingencies and provide guidelines for dealing with them.

Specific topics include (1) theory and theory building, (2) models for demonstration and applied research, (3) the structure of research organization, (4) managerial problems in social research, (5) design and administration of a research project, and (6) integration of research and practice.

Price, James L. *Organizational Effectiveness: An Inventory of Propositions.* Homewood, Ill., Richard D. Irwin, Inc., 1968. 212 pp.

Price consolidates the findings of behavioral science to produce a propositional inventory of the determinants of organizational effectiveness. The inventory is based on fifty organizational case studies by various scholars. Five variables that influence effectiveness (defined as the degree of goal achievement) are considered: productivity, morale, conformity, adaptiveness, and institutionalization.

The material is organized into four categories: (1) the economic system, (2) the political system, (3) the control system, and (4) population ecology. Each proposition is followed by a short discussion and definition of terms.

Some of the characteristics an effective organization is likely to exhibit are: high degrees of specialization; rational-legal decision making; autonomy, congruence, and conformity in the organization's external political system; and large size.

Rivlin, Alice M. *Systematic Thinking for Social Action.* Washington, D.C., Brookings Institution, 1971. 150 pp.

This is an examination of the contributions made by systems analysis to decision making in social-action programs. Four propositions summarize the contributions: (1) considerable progress has been made in identifying and measuring social problems in our society, (2) systematic analysis has improved our knowledge of the distribution of the initial costs and benefits of social-action programs, (3) little progress has been made in comparing the benefits of different social-action programs, (4) little is known about how to produce more effective health, education, and other social services.

The author believes that the federal government should take the lead in a wide application of social experimentation. Such a strategy requires (1) identifying new methods for delivering services, (2) systematically trying out these new methods in various places and under various conditions, and (3) evaluating these methods and comparing them with each other and with methods already in use. The final chapter deals with three models for improving the effectiveness of social services: decentralization, community control, and a market system. While all three models hold some promise, none is a cure-all. Rivlin concludes that effective functioning of social service systems depends on measure of achievement and suggests two general rules: (1) single measure of social service performance should be avoided, and (2) performance measure must reflect the difficulty of the problem.

Schulberg, Herbert C., Alan Sheldon, and Frank Baker, eds. *Program Evaluation in the Health Fields.* New York, Behavioral Publications, 1969. 582 pp.

Here is a comprehensive reference source for researchers and administrators concerned with the evaluation of health programs. The papers presented were selected on the basis of their relevance to issues faced by both professions.

Two major approaches to evaluation are described: the goal-attainment model and the systems model. Different research designs, methodological techniques, and evaluation indexes are cited, along with examples of evaluations of actual health programs. A section is devoted to problems of the final step in evaluation—putting the findings to work.

Most importantly, the administrator is apprised of the

complexities of program evaluation and is given advice on how to make realistic decisions about his own evaluation needs. Gaps between concepts and techniques are pointed out to enable the researcher to develop solutions to evaluation problems.

Somers, G. G., and W. D. Woods, eds. *Cost-Benefit Analysis of Manpower Policies.* Kingston, Ontario, Industrial Relations Center, Queens University, 1969. 272 pp.

This series of papers and discussions, presented at the North American Conference on Cost-Benefit Analysis of Manpower Policies in 1969, is arranged in two sections; the first dealing with the theoretical aspects of cost-benefit analysis, the second with its application to manpower programs. Among the issues examined in the first section are the objectives of manpower programs, the use of foregone or opportunity costs, the role of cost-benefit analysis in policy formulation, and the use of the social discount rate.

Turning from theoretical considerations, the second section examines the use of cost-benefit analysis in evaluating occupational-training programs, programs for training the disadvantaged, and the Canadian Manpower Mobility programs. A survey of cost-benefit studies of occupationally oriented, institutional training programs presents a comparison of the concepts and methods used in these studies, as well as a comparison of findings from the points of view of society, the individual trainee, and the government.

Suchman, Edward A. *Evaluative Research: Principles and Practice in Public Service and Social Action Programs.* New York, Russell Sage Foundation, 1967. 186 pp.

Suchman describes the techniques used to (1) empirically determine the extent to which social programs are achieving their goals, (2) identify the barriers to the achievement of these goals, and (3) discover the unanticipated consequences of social actions. The material is divided into three sections dealing with the conceptual, methodological, and administrative aspects of evaluation.

The author begins with a historical review of evaluative research and a look at the current status of evaluative studies, emphasizing the limitations of self-evaluation in community public service programs. The evaluation process is defined in terms of values, objectives, and assumptions. The section on methodology summarizes various approaches to evaluation and analyzes a number of research designs. The administrative aspects of evaluation explored are (1) the place of evaluation in the administrative process, (2) administrative resistance and barriers to evaluation, and (3) difficulties encountered in administering evaluation studies. The concluding chapter discusses the relationship of evaluative research to social experimentation.

Tripodi, Tony, Phillip Fellin, and Irwin Epstein. *Social Program Evaluation—Guidelines for Health, Education and Welfare Administrators*. Itasca, Ill., Peacock Publishers, 1971. 142 pp.

Ultimately a program director must take the responsibility for the evaluation of his program and the uses to which the results of that evaluation are put. The more knowledge the administrator has about program evaluation the greater role he can play in maximizing the relevance of the evaluation. The purpose of this book is to help the administrator decide whether his program should be evaluated, when this should be done, and what method should be used. Administrators in the fields of health, education, and welfare are provided guidelines to help them initiate and sustain evaluation studies.

The authors urge the application of "differentiated evaluation." This is an attempt to determine program efforts, effectiveness, and efficiency at three stages—program initiation, contact with the target population, and implementation. Evaluation objectives for health, education, and welfare programs are discussed, and information is given to aid in the determination of which evaluation technique is most appropriate to the objectives. Three classifications of techniques are outlined: monitoring techniques (accountability or administrative audits), cost-analysis techniques (cost benefit, cost accounting), and social research techniques (experiments, surveys). An annotated bibliography follows each of the three classifications.

Weiss, Carol H. *Evaluation Research: Methods of Assessing Program Effectiveness.* Englewood Cliffs, N.J., Prentice-Hall, Inc., 1972. 160 pp.

This practical text on social program evaluation espouses the theme that "evaluation uses the methods and tools of social research but applies them in an action context that is intrinsically inhospitable to them." Weiss examines the reasons, both overt and covert, for undertaking program evaluation and recommends that the evaluator tailor the study to the needs of the program's decision makers. She addresses the following issues in evaluation: identifying concrete program goals and choosing which to evaluate; unexpected consequences of programs; and identifying essential program elements and determining why the program succeeds or fails.

Sources for the collection of data for evaluation research are listed. A chapter on developing the evaluation design considers the experimental, quasi-experimental, and non-experimental designs; comparative program evaluation; cost-benefit analysis; and planning-programming-budgeting systems. The action setting of evaluation research and the problems it creates are presented, including the tendency of a program to change during evaluation, the relations between the evaluator and program personnel, and the effects of the program's social context. Constraints found to limit the utilization of evaluation results are (1) the academic orientation of most evaluators, (2) organizational resistance to change, (3) inadequate dissemination of evaluation results, (4) failure of the evaluation to indicate a clear course of desired program action, and (5) the tendency of many evaluations to determine few or no program results.

Wholey, Joseph S., et al. *Federal Evaluation Policy: Analyzing the Effects of Public Programs*. Washington, D.C., Urban Institute, 1970. 134 pp. (paperback).

The findings and recommendations presented in this study of federal evaluation policies before September, 1969, are as relevant today as they were when they were published. The authors examine the status of evaluation in fifteen social programs conducted by the Department of Health, Education, and Welfare, the Department of Housing and Urban Development, the Department of Labor, and the Office of Economic Opportunity. They find that substantial work in this field has been almost nonexistent. The most clear-cut evidence of the primitive state of federal evaluation is in the failure of most agencies to articulate program objectives.

This study sets forth what federal evaluation is and why it is needed; what functions an adequate evaluation system must perform; what roles Congress, the Executive branch, federal agencies, and state and local agencies play in establishing and shaping the federal evaluation system; what financial and in-house staff resources are needed to achieve sound evaluations of federal programs; and what the methodological issues are when an evaluation is carried out. A final chapter lists the major recommendations with regard to federal evaluation policy that emerged from the study. An extensive bibliography is included.

IV. PERSONNEL

"IF management means getting results through people, then management is nothing more than personnel administration" (L. A. Appley). Management is responsible for performing the functions by which the established goals of the organization are effectively and efficiently carried out. The effectiveness and efficiency of any organization depend in large measure on the ability of its management to properly select, develop, and utilize its human resources. The management of people is inherent in all organizations, and, although primary responsibility for personnel management rests at top management levels, certain responsibilities for personnel duties must be assumed and carried out at all levels of the organization.

Since the tasks, education, and skills of both the manager and his subordinates have become increasingly complex, today's manager at each level must have greater technical competence in the management of people. Personnel management is the function that encompasses, among other things, the recruiting, selection, placement, training, orientation, evaluation, and promotion of all individuals engaged in the activities of the organization regardless of their role and function.

This section of the bibliography includes not only material dealing with traditional personnel administration but also the two additional areas that reflect new and important concerns in the management of people: collective bargaining and manpower.

Passive, politically neutral public employees are an endangered species. Increasing numbers of public employees are organizing, bargaining, striking, and demanding a larger role in affairs traditionally the concern of management alone. Organized public employees and the collective bargaining process represent a new challenge for public administrators, demanding a new perspective, new knowledge, and new skills. The literature of collective bargaining cannot give easy answers for resolving union-management conflicts. It can, however, give fresh perspectives on the issues, procedures, and legal and historical backgrounds and can report the effects of public employee organizations on public administration.

Manpower policy and planning originally reflected a national perspective and sought the best use of all the nation's human resources. Jobs and job requirements also change in the organization and its immediate environment, and the social turmoil of the 1960's forced a reexamination of the social responsibility of business to help train and employ the disadvantaged. New skills, new machines, and new social priorities can make jobs obsolete. Now social service organizations, concerned with rehabilitating or retraining the unemployed or disadvantaged, must have knowledge of regional, if not national, manpower needs so that the client will be trained for a job that actually exists—a job not doomed by technology to become extinct.

The effective use of human resources is the most challenging and difficult aspect of the management process. The future of any organization depends on the success with which management is able to tap and release the energy, ability, skill, and enthusiasm of its employees. Few are willing to admit that they do not understand people, and yet this lack of understanding is everywhere apparent and leads to the wrong choice of employees, poor employee relations, inadequate production, general employee discontent, worker alienation, and strikes. Revolutionary forces are challenging the traditional concepts and practices of management. Employees are becoming highly articulate, insisting on more purposeful work and demanding a greater voice in the affairs of the organization. The selections in this section are addressed to the manager who desires to better equip himself to deal effectively with the human problems of his organization.

A. Personnel Management

Barrett, Richard S. *Performance Rating.* Chicago, Science Research Associates, Inc., 1966. 166 pp.

This book is intended to help managers evaluate the performance of all personnel. The author gives the following uses of performance rating: to develop programs of wage and salary administration; to determine who is to be promoted, transferred, laid off, or demoted; and to provide administrative control. Barrett emphasizes that an effective performance-rating program should have employee acceptance, relevance, and variability. Various methods of performance rating are discussed, including graphic rating, ranking, forced choice, and critical-incident techniques. Barrett emphasizes that the performance-rating responsibility should be assigned to the most suitable "rater," and he describes techniques for improving performance ratings through the training and supervision of the raters.

Bassett, Glenn A., and Harvard Y. Weatherbee. *Personnel Systems and Data Management.* New York, American Management Association, Inc., 1971. 242 pp.

Designed for personnel specialists, this is a nontechnical introduction to the use of computers and systems analysis to generate improved personnel information. The book deals with different techniques of gathering, developing, manipulating, and storing personnel data and for solving the problems encountered in implementing and managing a computerized personnel system. Included is an introduction to GEDAN, a computer-programming language using English commands, and samples of data-base questionnaires, punch-card instruction sheets, and GEDAN programs for developing practical information from personnel data.

Beach, Dale S. *Managing People at Work: Readings in Personnel.* New York, Macmillan Company, 1971. 516 pp.

Covering the principal issues in personnel management and organizational behavior, the articles in this collection are directed both to the student and to those administrators who want to keep up with current trends in the field. The material is drawn from journals, conference proceedings, monographs, and research reports that the reader would not normally encounter. The range of topics is broad and includes articles that summarize current behavioral-science research and important philosophical and ethical issues. Certain articles challenge conventional points of view. In addition to predictable articles dealing with organizations and the personnel function, topics of special interest include employing the culturally deprived, discipline and grievance handling in administrative justice, safety and mental health, collective bargaining, and social responsibility.

Fear, Richard A. *The Evaluation Interview.* 2d ed. New York, McGraw-Hill Book Company, 1973. 320 pp.

Written by a practitioner, this is a comprehensive book about fitting the right man to the right job through the employment interview. The author provides step-by-step procedures for conducting the interview from the time the job applicant walks in the door to the writing of the interview report.

Discussion of the selection process begins with a description of screening techniques, such as selective recruiting, job specifications, testing, and the preliminary interview. The author shows how to use a final patterned interview to appraise the personality, motivation, interests, character, and nature of intellectual functioning of the job applicant. Emphasis is given to the importance of establishing a rapport with the applicant so that he will be encouraged to talk spontaneously. Guidelines are presented to help the interviewer launch discussion into important job areas, keep the applicant talking, and guide the discussion to the most relevant matters. Suggestions are made on how to interpret the results of the interview in light of the applicant's work history, education, home background, present social adjustment, self-evaluation, and key personality traits. Three factors are listed that should take precedence over all others in the final consideration of the applicant's qualifications: mental ability, motivation, and maturity.

Appendices include an interview guide, which structures areas to be explored and specific items to be covered during the interview, an interview rating form, and illustrative reports of interview findings.

French, Wendell. *The Personnel Management Process.* 3d ed. Boston, Houghton Mifflin Company, 1974. 756 pp.

The author views personnel management as a network of interrelated, dynamic processes within any organization and analyzes in detail nine interdependent processes: leadership, justice determination, task specialization, staffing, performance appraisal, training and development, compensation and reward, collective bargaining, and organization development. French contends that all managers are, in fact, personnel managers and that the nine identified processes are found in most organizations. This approach provides the framework for an analysis of personnel-management functions from the viewpoint of the total organization. Extensive use is made of behavioral science, particularly psychology. Current personnel practices and significant personnel research are summarized. The appendix provides a comprehensive yet concise chronological history of personnel management in the United States.

Otto, Calvin P., and Rollin O. Glaser. *The Management of Training: A Handbook for Training and Development*

Personnel. Reading, Mass., Addison-Wesley Publishing Company, Inc., 1970. 410 pp.

This source book of basic information about the management of training concentrates on the fundamentals of the training job with pragmatic solutions to training problems. Using a how-to approach, the handbook provides a foundation from which to plan, develop, administer, and evaluate an effective training program while operating within real budget, time, and staff limits.

The handbook describes the application of training principles and equipment in different organizational training settings, including orientation for new employees, job instruction, training for supervisors, and management development. Topics include a description of a training director's job; the selection and training of an instructional staff; techniques for analyzing training problems, developing training objectives, and building the course programs and lessons; buying and using equipment effectively; and evaluating the outcome of training.

Pigors, Paul, and Charles A. Myers. *Personnel Administration: A Point of View and a Method.* 7th ed. New York, McGraw-Hill Book Company, 1973. 588 pp.

This edition presents the authors' views of personnel administration and a method for making it work. It includes recent research in the behavioral sciences and developments in the field but retains the point of view of earlier editions. The authors describe differing management philosophies but emphasize the line managers' responsibility to coordinate and utilize personnel under their leadership. The control function is discussed, and insights are given into management development through changes in organization structure, manpower planning, performance appraisal, and self-development. Communication is seen as an integral part of management's responsibility in personnel administration, and motivation, individual goals, and teamwork are discussed.

The section on method deals with the skills necessary for diagnosing organizational ills. The authors stress that the administrator must be able to apply situational thinking to obtain a relatively objective outlook of the situation while also developing the skills to conduct interviews, handle complaints, and evaluate performance.

Pigors and Myers examine concepts of development and utilization of human resources, including the establishment of policies for recruitment and hiring. They believe that these policies should be designed to aid the employee in various stages of growth within the organization. The book concludes with nineteen illustrative cases.

Stahl, O. Glenn. *The Personnel Job of Government Managers*. Chicago, Public Personnel Association, 1971. 186 pp.

Stahl believes that knowledge of the personnel function is a principal—and heretofore ignored—component of every government manager's job. Stahl gives a detailed discussion of what government managers need to know and what they have to do in the areas where personnel management is mainly practiced—assignment and supervision of people, teaching and leading staff members, and holding workers to high standards of performance. The success of a government manager depends on the effective use of his people, and he is as responsible for developing and implementing personnel policies as is the personnel specialist.

Stahl deals with leadership and employee relations, the responsibility of the leader to motivate, the organization and assignment of work, and the executive's responsibility for dealing with unions. The best practices that have evolved in each area of managerial responsibilities are discussed.

Stahl, O. Glenn. *Public Personnel Administration.* 6th ed. New York, Harper & Row, Inc., 1971. 502 pp.

This revised edition of a classic brings together experience and research in public personnel administration. The function of personnel administration is defined broadly as the "totality of concern with the human resources of an organization." Personnel administration is seen as an important link between the organization and its environment. Stahl believes that the increased size of government and social changes make it imperative that basic value orientation—work-centered motivation, the merit concept, and high standards of employee performance—be maintained.

Topics include examination, selection, motivation, evaluation, development, separation, and ethics. There is a short section on public personnel administration around the world, and the book includes a good, partially annotated bibliography organized by topic and chapter. For the public administrator the book is useful as a compilation of current thinking and practice.

Warren, Malcolm W. *Training for Results: A Systems Approach to the Development of Human Resources in Industry.* Reading, Mass., Addison-Wesley Publishing Company, Inc., 1969. 240 pp.

This book provides carefully charted procedures for developing a training system and preparing an effective training program within the system. The major emphasis is on results and a good economic return on the training investment. The training system is developed by examining its five key elements: research; analysis of objectives, criteria, and constraints in the training plan; development of specific training actions; implementation of the training plan; and evaluation of the training plan and the trainees' performance. Individual chapters are devoted to six training program areas: industrial skills, administrative skills, sales, induction orientation, professional and technical training, and management and supervisory training.

B. Manpower

Conley, Ronald W. *The Economics of Vocational Rehabilitation*. Baltimore, Johns Hopkins University Press, 1965. 178 pp.

Although it was written nearly a decade ago, this book remains one of the best introductions to the economics of vocational rehabilitation (VR). As an investigation into selected aspects of the economic problems caused by disability, both physical and mental, and of the benefits of vocational rehabilitation, it deals with the characteristics and costs of disability, the economic evaluation of the VR program, and the history of VR in the United States. This study produced five major conclusions: (1) disability is a large and important problem, and the costs in terms of well-being and services are staggering, (2) many disabled persons can be treated and retrained at an over-all savings to society and the taxpayers, (3) adverse attitudes of the disabled and employers are major hindrances to rehabilitation, (4) returns per dollar spent for services for the less productive rehabilitants are about as great as the returns for those who are more productive, and (5) the rehabilitation program should be expanded so as to help more disabled persons into gainful employment. A concluding section concerns the important issue of whether more persons should be rehabilitated. Here the author develops a theory of providing rehabilitative services and discusses the unmet vocational needs of the handicapped, the requirements for an optimal VR program, and the earnings and costs of an expanding program.

Doeringer, Peter B., ed. *Programs to Employ the Disadvantaged.* Englewood Cliffs, N. J., Prentice-Hall, Inc., 1969. 262 pp.

An examination and comparison of programs by management, labor, government, and civil-rights groups to provide job opportunities for the disadvantaged. Nine case studies in manpower were selected to represent a variety of problems and approaches. The major emphasis is on the private sector, including manpower experiences of Western Electric, IBM, Westinghouse, the Equitable Life Assurance Society, and the Cooperative Steel Industry Education Program. Other projects described are the Woodland Job Training Center, the Worker's Defense League Pre-Apprenticeship Training Program, Department of Defense Project 100,000, and the Concentrated Employment Program of Boston's Community Action Agency. Each section contains a description of the manpower program and a subsequent discussion of the program's implications and lessons.

Joint Commission on Correctional Manpower and Training. *Perspectives on Correctional Manpower and Training.* Washington, D.C., Joint Commission on Correctional Manpower and Training, 1970. 158 pp. Galvin, John J., and Loren Karacki. *Manpower and Training in Correctional Institutions.* Washington, D.C., Joint Commission on Correctional Manpower and Training, 1969. 88 pp. Nelson, Elmer K., and Catherine H. Lovell. *Developing Correctional Administrators.* Washington, D.C., Joint Commission on Correctional Manpower and Training, 1969. 162 pp.

Perspectives on Correctional Manpower and Training is an overview of contemporary manpower corrections programs. It discusses barriers to change in corrections, the need for specialized manpower in corrections, new concepts in parole and probation, the use of volunteer workers in correctional institutions, recruitment problems, personnel policies, and maximization of potential manpower resources.

Manpower and Training in Correctional Institutions presents a broad examination of adult and juvenile correctional institutions. The authors stress the need for planning in and for correctional facilities and the need for more cooperation between institutional employees and inmates.

Developing Correctional Administrators describes the characteristics, behavior, and attitudes of juvenile and adult correctional administrators, the problems administrators encounter, and the skills they need to perform their duties. The report urges greater use of participative techniques in correctional management and makes suggestions for the improvement of administration in correctional institutions.

Levitan, Sar A., Garth L. Mangum, and Ray Marshall. *Human Resources and Labor Markets: Labor and Manpower in the American Economy.* New York, Harper & Row, Publishers, Inc., 1972. 620 pp.

This integration of human resource development, labor-market economics, and economic theory concentrates on five basic areas: (1) the factors that affect the supply and demand for labor; (2) how workers are allocated among jobs and jobs among workers; (3) productivity of the work force; (4) how efficiently labor-market institutions utilize available human resources, and (5) the role of public and private policy in the labor market.

The result is a historical and critical review of manpower theory and practices in dealing with basic labor problems and pathologies: unemployment, underemployment, and discrimination. The authors conclude that no comprehensive human-resources policy exists in the United States and that it is not clear that such a policy would be desirable or necessary. What is clear is that human-resource policies and practices must be flexible and that steps can be taken to increase the adaptability of human-resources policy to the changes that lie ahead. This book is a thorough but basic introduction to manpower management. An annotated bibliography is included.

Mangum, Garth L. *MDTA: Foundation of Federal Manpower Policy*. Baltimore, Johns Hopkins University Press, 1968. 184 pp.

Mangum traces the political and legislative evolution of the Manpower Development and Training Act (MDTA) of 1962 and evaluates the program as it actually functioned. The rationale for the original act was that job vacancies could be filled and unemployment reduced by training the unemployed to fill the job vacancies. While this original goal was not reached, Mangum says that other accomplishments of MDTA have made it a prudent investment of public funds. These other accomplishments include raising the visibility and status of manpower policy in government and developing new tools for serving the disadvantaged through MDTA's experimental and demonstrative projects.

MDTA's research funds developed new information, helped shift the attention of labor economists from industrial relations to manpower problems, and spurred efforts to encourage lethargic institutions to serve population groups they had previously ignored. The experience gained from MDTA influenced subsequent employment, antipoverty, and manpower training programs.

Mangum also discusses the unresolved issues of MDTA: (1) whether MDTA should seek to upgrade the labor force or rehabilitate the disadvantaged; (2) the relative advantages of institutional versus on-the-job training; (3) the role and relationship of federal and local governments in determining policy and operations; and (4) whether a permanent MDTA program is needed, and if so, what its nature and size should be.

Mangum, Garth L., and Lowell M. Glenn. *Vocational Rehabilitation and Federal Manpower Policy*. Ann Arbor, Institute of Labor and Industrial Relations, 1967. 58 pp.

This book attempts to determine what the federal manpower programs could learn from the vocational rehabilitation delivery system. The authors briefly trace the history and politics of vocational rehabilitation and outline the program as it stands today. Some of the areas treated are services (evaluation and counseling, medical aid, education and training, work experiences), the counselor and client characteristics, and client selection.

Lessons learned from vocational rehabilitation fall into three major categories: the economic benefits of vocational rehabilitation for society, the need for interagency coordination, and the comprehensive approach to manpower services. Significant findings in the three categories are (1) regardless of the great differences in estimates of benefit-cost ratios, there is a high return for the public funds invested in vocational rehabilitation; (2) although the Rehabilitation Services Administration has not felt much need to use the services of other agencies, vocational rehabilitation has willingly provided services to these agencies, especially in client education, and (3) there are great advantages in vocational rehabilitation's comprehensive approach, which has few limits on the services that can be provided or the kinds of clients who can be served.

The Institute of Labor and Industrial Relations is a joint arrangement of the University of Michigan and Wayne State University. The institute has published a series of policy papers dealing primarily with programs in manpower, education, employment, and poverty. The papers generally are brief, to the point, and readable. Examples are *Antipoverty Work and Training Efforts: Goals and Reality,* by Sar A. Levitan (1970); *Jobs and Income for Negroes*, by Charles C. Killingsworth (1968); *Job Development for the Hard-to-Employ*, by Louis A. Ferman (1969); *Employing the Disadvantaged in the Federal Civil Service*, by Garth L. Mangum and Lowell M. Glenn (1969); *Education for Employment: The Background and Potential of the 1968 Vocational Education Amendments*, by Rupert N. Evans, Garth L. Mangum, and Otto Pragan (1969).

Sartain, Aaron Q., and Alton W. Baker. *The Supervisor*

and His Job. New York, McGraw-Hill Book Company, 1965. 464 pp.

This book describes fundamental and practical concepts for the first-line supervisor, emphasizing his major functions, the critical importance of his interpersonal relationships, and his ethical, emotional, and intellectual development. A central theme is that effective supervision is not primarily a function of what a supervisor does but depends on the kind of person the supervisor is taken to be and in most cases the kind of person he actually is. The book is addressed to three classes of readers: those who aspire to be supervisors, those who are currently supervisors, and those who manage first-line supervisors. Topics discussed include productivity, worker attitudes and motivation, work simplification, development and compensation of subordinates, counseling, communication, and the evaluation and discipline of subordinates.

Somers, Gerald G., ed. *Retraining the Unemployed.* Madison, University of Wisconsin Press, 1968. 352 pp.

A series of evaluative studies of geographically scattered federal, state, municipal, and union-management training programs attempting to determine whether or not trainees find jobs and how much of the success in finding jobs can be attributed to the retraining programs. The major conclusions of these studies are as follows:

1. Retraining programs for unemployed workers are sound social investments. In most of the programs analyzed, 75 per cent or more of the participants gained employment after their training.

2. Retraining programs have raised the economic position of the trainees. Their earnings after training rose significantly over their earlier earnings and over the earnings of nontrainees.

3. Society as a whole benefits from retraining programs

inasmuch as they increase tax revenues and reduce assistance payments.

4. The cost of retraining programs to participants and society can be readily recovered.

5. Social gains, in the form of improvements in morale, self-esteem, and social status, can be inferred from the data.

In those studies where employers were interviewed, a significant proportion of them mentioned the importance of the trainee's general characteristics, rather than his newly acquired skill, in hiring practices. In the studies using regression analysis, retraining was shown to be of more significance for successful employment in the labor market than such variables as age, sex, race, education, marital status, and labor-market area. A bibliographical appendix on retraining the unemployed is included.

Work in America. Report of a Special Task Force to the Secretary of Health, Education, and Welfare, prepared by the W. E. Upjohn Institute for Employment Research. Cambridge, Mass., M.I.T. Press, 1973. 262 pp.

This report is an extensive exploration of the adverse economic, social, and personal consequences of work dissatisfaction. It stresses the need for a concerted effort to redesign jobs in order to give the worker more control of his immediate work environment and thus enhance his self-esteem and importance. The obstacles to the redesigning of jobs and the deficiencies of government policy in the creation of jobs, manpower training, and welfare are discussed and alternative strategies suggested. Thirty-four documented efforts to redesign jobs in the United States and several foreign countries are included, with special attention given to both the personal and the economic consequences of the efforts to humanize the job environment.

C. Collective Bargaining

Bloom, Gordon F., and Herbert R. Northrup. *Economics of Labor Relations.* 7th ed. Homewood, Ill., Richard D. Irwin, Inc., 1973. 772 pp.

This comprehensive discussion of labor relations and collective bargaining emphasizes issues that currently dominate labor relations. Following an introduction to the study of labor relations, the book deals with labor history, union structure, collective-bargaining techniques, the role of government in collective bargaining, and manpower planning and collective bargaining in the public sector. Particular attention is given to the Occupational Safety and Health Act of 1970, federal and state labor legislation, and public-employee unionism.

The current issues of unemployment, poverty, race relations, inflation, environmental concerns, and public unionism are treated in detail. In the final chapter the authors deal with the future role of unions in the American economy and note some important labor problems. Questions are raised about the impact of employee excesses in collective bargaining, the inconsistency of federal legislation, and the failure of industrial unions to grow. The authors conclude that "there is a real need for a general overhauling of our disjointed system of conflicting and overlapping labor laws."

Davey, Harold W. *Contemporary Collective Bargaining.* 3d ed. Englewood Cliffs, N.J., Prentice-Hall, Inc., 1972. 402 pp.

More a new book than a new edition, this work focuses on issues, needs, and problems encountered by practitioners of collective bargaining but does not neglect the academic requirements of students of the process. The book deals candidly with current critical labor relations, problems, and issues: new chapters on public-sector labor relations and an extensive discussion of wage-price guidelines and their effect on the collective bargaining process are included.

Other topics covered are: (1) the public policy framework for collective bargaining, (2) principles, problems, and procedures of contract negotiation, (3) contract administration, (4) grievance arbitration, (5) resolution of future term disputes, (6) job security and industrial jurisprudence, (7) collective bargaining and microeconomic aspects, (8) negotiated economic security packages and other fringe benefits, and (9) bargaining by government and professional employees.

Davey is a pragmatist; he calls collective bargaining an "imperfect institutional process that works reasonably well in an imperfect society." He closes with a plea for labor and management to develop a "trilateral perspective," that is, to adapt their private decision making to public-policy goals. Otherwise, Davey says, there is no guarantee for the continued privacy of collective bargaining.

Heisel, W. D., and J. D. Hallihan. *Questions and Answers on Public Employee Negotiation.* Chicago, Public Personnel Association, 1967. 214 pp.

Written by practitioners, this guide to the techniques and issues in labor relations should prove useful to negotiating and bargaining participants.

The information, arranged in a question-and-answer format, is ideal for quick reference and deals with specific issues and practical problems in the negotiation process.

Since the writers see conflict in the labor-management relationship as inevitable, they concentrate on clarifying and settling disputes rather than avoiding them. Topics include (1) basic principles, strategies and tactics of management during bargaining, (2) procedures for negotiation and breaking impasses, (3) subjects included in bargaining and subjects not generally negotiable, and (4) the writing of the contract with examples of language included.

Labor-management relationships away from the bargaining table are also covered: (1) establishing the relationship, (2) ordinary labor-management concerns, such as grievance procedures and discipline, and (3) the legal aspects of labor-management relations.

Nigro, Felix A. *Management-Employee Relations in the Public Service.* Chicago, Public Personnel Association, 1969. 434 pp.

Nigro analyzes the basic issues and problems in developing a successful joint relationship between employee unions and public management. This noted practitioner and scholar sees bargaining as "flexible maneuver, not battle from fixed position," with the long-term goal of creating the conditions in which public employees will not want to strike.

The thorny political issues of sovereignty and authority and the effects of bargaining on the merit system are explored, with examples of working resolutions from both the United States and Canada. Key policy issues of bargaining rights, union shops, the right to organize, definitions of essential services for determining the right to strike, and antistrike legislation—all the significant elements in the bargaining environment—are included. The scope and conduct of actual negotiations, including mediation, fact finding, arbitration, and impasse and grievance-settling procedures round out the narrative portion of the book. An appendix includes a lengthy list of subjects appropriate for negotiation and resource materials on grievance and evaluation procedures.

Stagner, Ross, and Hjalmar Rosen. *Psychology of Union-Management Relations.* Behavioral Science in Industry

Series. Belmont, Calif., Brooks/Cole Publishing Company, 1965. 148 pp.

This book investigates the psychological processes within the human personality that contribute to the occurrence of disputes between union and management. The treatment is neutral toward the values of managers and unionists but reveals how different ways of looking at situations and the differing goals of union and management can lead to conflict. Theories of individual perception and motivation are developed and used to analyze the ways in which the organizational structures of the company and the union modify individual motivations and perceptions. The book also emphasizes how the knowledge of the psychology of individual perception and motivation can be used to help settle or forestall disputes by improving the sensitivity of leadership and by improving communications between unions and management.

Stanley, David T., with Carole L. Cooper. *Managing Government Under Union Pressure.* Washington, D.C., Brookings Institution, 1972. 178 pp.

This report concentrates on the major patterns of change in public administration resulting from union activities. It finds that, in local government, both legislative bodies and chief executives have become more preoccupied with union matters and more limited in their discretion to manage. The reason is primarily the political power of public unions, and this report centers attention on their influence on hiring, promotions, training, job classification, pay, benefits, work management and working conditions, and local budgets and finance. The report concludes that public administration is undergoing major changes leading to more bilateral decision making as a result of union pressures and counsels public managers to accept the fact of unionism and use their energies to build and maintain a sound legal framework for union relations. A selected bibliography is included.

Stieber, Jack. *Public Employee Unionism: Structure, Growth, Policy.* Studies of Unionism in Government Series. Washington, D.C., Brookings Institution, 1973. 256 pp.

Public and industrial unions differ, and this book focuses on the distinctive aspects of organization and bargaining in public employment at the state and local levels. Its content was developed from primary sources and personal interviews with clerical workers, police, firemen, nurses, the American Federation of State, County and Municipal Employees, and others.

The wide variety of employee organizations—public unions and mixed unions, as well as employee, professional, occupational and uniformed associations—are compared in terms of their organization, structure, leadership, staff support, finances, and minority group participation. The bases of conflict and cooperation within public-employee organizations and within industrial unions are examined with respect to different attitudes toward collective bargaining, determination of bargaining units, representation elections, the strike issue, and the extent and form of political activity. Past union studies have concentrated on industrial unions. The growth of public-employee organizations and collective bargaining in the last decade has created a need for increased knowledge and understanding of the organizations—both union and nonunion—that represent public employees. This book is a step in that direction.

Wykstra, Ronald A., and Eleanour V. Stevens. *Labor Law and Public Policy.* New York, Odyssey Press, 1970. 452 pp.

This textbook on labor law offers a concise historical review of the labor legislation, judicial decisions, and public policies that determine the legal boundaries of the area in which labor and management interact. The narrative is extensively illustrated with excerpts from court opinions, National Labor Relations Board decisions, and public laws. Although the historical treatment necessarily includes a large amount of material on industrial unions, two chapters deal with legal issues for public employees and human-resource utilization. Special attention is also given to national emergency strikes, the weapons of conflict, collective bargaining, and manpower policy. Appendices include the body of major legislative acts referred to in the text.

V. THE ADMINISTRATIVE ENVIRONMENT

Public administration does not occur in a closet — the people's business is conducted in the public arena. The conduct of administration is influenced by its environment, which includes broad social values and attitudes, the clients served by the organization, the wider notion of public interest, and political and economic power. To a considerable degree the effectiveness of a public administrator depends on his sensitivity to and awareness of the ideas, persons, and institutions that influence public policy and set priorities.

The purpose of public administration is to serve people; thus the client population and the general public are vital elements in the environment of public administration. A public organization is an important link between the people and their government, and the quality of that relationship is a good measure of how well the organization achieves its service objectives. Public relations built on propaganda or secrecy creates indifference or suspicion; but open, two-way communication can create public understanding and support for programs while alerting administrators to special problems of service delivery. If administrators know the facts, tell the truth, and listen, public relations can result in a positive image based on service rather than self-serving rhetoric. The books included in the "Public Relations" section show how to establish an effective public relations program and furnish practical suggestions on the use of various media for public and clientele communication.

Public administration operates within a political system composed of many interacting and competing groups, and, although public administrators play an important role as formulators and implementers of public policy, their influence is only part of a larger process. The political process by which public policy is formulated, enacted, and implemented is long and complex. Knowledge of the political process—of *who* makes public policy decisions and *how* they are made—is necessary if the administrator is to be one of the participants in that process. The selections in "Public Policy" stress the role of public administration in the American political process.

Intergovernmental relations in the American federal system are an important aspect of the job of the effective public administrator. In their work public employees are routinely in touch with operations at the federal, state, or local levels. Ideally, the federal system should function in a vigorous, dynamic, and cooperative equilibrium. But the federal system is a complex environment, especially in direct federal-local relations, categorical grants-in-aid, and revenue sharing. The books in this section view the intergovernmental environment from the perspective of various levels of government; analyze the federal grant-in-aid, an important administrative technique in intergovernmental relations; and discuss the problems of administering federal aid programs and revenue sharing. The intent is to provide the administrator with a better understanding of the workings of the American federal system.

Science and technology change our material lives and alter personal and social values. The basic values the administrator brings to his job and the values of those he works for strongly influence the means and ends of his labor, even when these values are not clearly articulated. The books in the "Values, Technology and Administration" section explore the nature of values and technology and the impact they have on public administration and society in general.

A. Public Relations

Cutlip, Scott M., and Allen H. Center. *Effective Public Relations*. 4th ed. Englewood Cliffs, N.J., Prentice-Hall, Inc., 1971. 702 pp.

This book presents a comprehensive overview of the field of public relations. The authors discuss the concept and development of public relations, including its historical background, its current state, the status of the practitioner, and the environment of public relations. An examination of the public relations process and how it should work is followed by a survey of the tools of communication. The printed word, spoken word, images, staged events, and principles of media relations are considered. The practice of public relations in specific areas is described, including businesses, professional societies, welfare agencies, and foreign countries. The authors conclude with optimistic predictions about the future of public relations as a profession.

Katz, Elihu, and Brenda Danet, eds. *Bureaucracy and the Public: A Reader in Official-Client Relations*. New York, Basic Books, Inc., 1973. 534 pp.

This collection of readings explores the interactions between bureaucratic officials and their clients in various organizational settings. The work combines two points of view—that of the social critic and that of the social scientist. Section I examines three elements of the organization's social environment: culture, community, and individual personalities. Section II contains selections concerned with organizational influences on official-client relations: goals, roles, and structures. Section III discusses situational influences in the physical and social setting of the official-client contact. Section IV reflects on problems raised in the preceding readings and suggests what can be done about them to make organizations work for people. More effective channels for client redress, the ombudsman, community mobilization, and the poverty lawyer are suggested as strategies for improvement. Clients of such diverse organizations as correctional institutions, public welfare agencies, social security, police, and customs are treated. Selections include both new material and classic studies of official-client relations.

Lerbinger, Otto, and Albert J. Sullivan, eds. *Information, Influence, and Communication: A Reader in Public Relations.* New York, Basic Books, Inc., 1965. 514 pp.

This is a compilation of articles describing the nature and scope of public relations and communications. The political, economic, and social spheres in which public relations are conducted are discussed. The four elements of the communication process—information, influence, impact, and empathy—are identified and explained. Articles also treat such issues in public relations as ethics, privacy, and social responsibility. Recommendations for further readings are made at successive stages in the book.

Roalman, Arthur R. *Profitable Public Relations.* Homewood, Ill., Dow-Jones-Irwin, Inc., 1968. 240 pp.

Written by a practitioner, this work is intended for managers who are not directly responsible for public relations within their organizations. It emphasizes the practical aspects of public relations. The author believes that successful public relations can be achieved by obtaining skilled, able personnel who can match the program objectives of public relations to over-all organizational goals. Public relations does not conform to any formula but must be related to the public mood. Topics covered are (1) how to find able and experienced public relations people, (2) how to avoid wasting public relations dollars, (3) how to use public relations to improve marketing and recruiting programs, (4) how to achieve effective public relations with Washington, how to obtain it, and what it costs, (5) lobbying at the state capitol, and (6) how to maintain good press relations. Twelve case studies, concerned with successful companies, profitable public relations activities, and wasteful public relations, are included.

Schmidt, Frances, and Harold N. Weiner, eds. *Public Relations in Health and Welfare.* New York, Columbia University Press, 1966. 278 pp.

A book of readings on the public-relations roles of persons involved in health and welfare organizations. The authors urge clarification of the objectives and images of health and welfare agencies and cooperation between these organizations to make public relations more effective. Some of the specific areas addressed are (1) the public image of the agency, (2) the public relations functions of the administrator and staff, (3) public relations for the client, (4) interagency public relations, (5) mass communications, and (6) public relations in government agencies. The authors are experts in public relations in the social welfare field.

Schwartz, James W., ed. *The Publicity Process.* Ames, Iowa State University Press, 1966. 286 pp.

The articles in this collection were chosen because of their practical applicability to the publicity process. Some of the topics covered are effective communications methods, the development of news stories, use of various media, and writing and advertising techniques. Many of the publicity concepts are pictorially illustrated.

B. Public Policy

Bailey, Stephen K., and Edith K. Mosher. *ESEA: The Office of Education Administers a Law*. Syracuse, Syracuse University Press, 1968. 394 pp.

A thorough examination of how the United States Office of Education implemented and was affected by the Elementary and Secondary Education Act (ESEA) of 1965. The book begins with a survey of legislative history leading to the passage of the ESEA and then turns to the enactment of the bill itself and discusses the specific features of each of its titles and several general provisions that had an important bearing on its acceptance. The authors also give an account of the reorganization of the United States Office of Education (USOE) in preparation for the execution of ESEA and analyze in detail the methods used to enforce and develop the new educational policies, emphasizing the absence of effective means to evaluate USOE programs. Results from a sampling of opinions of state and local education offices are included.

Barone, Michael, Grant Ujifusa, and Douglas Matthews. *The Almanac of American Politics: The Senators, the Representatives— Their Records, States, and Districts*. Boston, Gambit, 1974. 1240 pp.

This biannual publication will prove useful to anyone interested in American public policy. Clearly written and supported by a wealth of statistical data, it is an excellent reference work on the political activities and backgrounds of the members of Congress and their respective states and districts. There is a basic dossier on each legislator, assembled into five parts: a biography and history of the career of the individual, the committees he serves on, political ratings by various interest groups, his voting record on key issues, and recent primary and general election results. The political background and environment of each state and congressional district are examined through census data, voting profiles, ethnic groups, federal expenditures in the area, and the district's economic base.

Dye, Thomas R. *Understanding Public Policy*. Englewood Cliffs, N.J., Prentice-Hall, Inc., 1972. 306 pp.

Dye's concern is with what public policies the American government pursues, why these policies are chosen, and what their consequences are. Six analytic models—systems, elite-mass, group, rational, incremental, and institutional—are employed to analyze public policy in a number of domestic areas: (1) civil rights, (2) violence and repression in the ghettos, (3) welfare and social security, (4) poverty and economic opportunity, (5) education, urban affairs, and housing, (6) government spending, budgeting and taxing, and (7) state and local spending and services. Results of the applications of the models and other recent research efforts are used to develop general propositions about how political processes and political behavior affect policy content and to assess the impact of policy on society.

Eidenburg, Eugene, and Roy D. Morey. *An Act of Congress: The Legislative Process and the Making of Educational Policy*. New York, W.W. Norton and Company, Inc., 1969. 256 pp.

A working description of the American policy-making process, centering on the issue of federal aid to education. The book deals with the events preceding the passage of the Elementary and Secondary Education Act of 1965, the passage of that act, and its subsequent modifications in 1966 and 1967. The authors examine the strategy to (1) overcome the religious controversy, (2) associate the bill with the then-popular antipoverty drive, and (3) ensure the bill's passage without amendment. The book is divided into three major sections. Part I presents a brief description of American public policy making, a historical look at federal aid to education before 1965, and the major changes in national politics after Kennedy's assassination up to the time of the Eighty-ninth Congress. Part II is devoted to a detailed study of ESEA. Part III surveys the modifications of the act in 1966 and 1967. The authors comment on the relative weight of public opinion, private groups, constituency, the news media, bureaucracies, the presidency, outside experts, congressional staff, and members and committees of Congress. An extensive use of interviews makes this a highly informative book.

Freeman, Howard E., and Clarence C. Sherwood. *Social Research and Social Policy*. Englewood Cliffs, N.J., Prentice-Hall, Inc., 1970. 160 pp.

Freeman thinks that the social scientist should direct his work toward the solution of contemporary social problems. The aim of the book is to (1) describe what the social-policy researcher does, (2) indicate some of the more important and useful perspectives, skills, and techniques of social-policy research, and (3) inform the reader about some of the major pitfalls and problems that occur when the social scientist elects a social-policy orientation.

After a discussion of the policy-making process, the roles of the policy researcher, and the historical development of social-policy research, the authors present the major technical activities of policy-oriented researchers. They relate research to planning, evaluation of program development, and data collection and analysis. They demonstrate that a rational planning process requires descriptive data on conditions and goals: that program development and implementation require development of an impact model and identification of target population and that evaluation requires assessing the execution of a program as a descriptive task and measuring program impact as a causal task. A concluding chapter discusses the interpersonal and nontechnical aspects of a social researcher's job, such as administrative and ethical concerns, personal conduct, and location and securing of financial support.

Lindblom, Charles E. *The Policy-making Process*. Englewood Cliffs, N.J., Prentice-Hall, Inc., 1968. 122 pp.

An analysis of how public policy decisions are made and implemented in America. Lindblom conceives of the policy-making process as a ladder, with the participants arrayed from the chief executive at the top to the ordinary citizens at the bottom. Opinions and preferences run up and down the ladder, each participant affecting, and responding to, the opinions and preferences of the others.

The author sees policy making as an extremely complex analytical and political process, which, owing to certain limitations, can reach beyond the competence of man. He identifies these limitations as (1) definition of the problem, (2) the complexity of the problem, time limits, and costs, (3) disagreement about values guiding policy selection, and (4) human resistance to policy analysis. Since policy can never be made in a perfectly correct way, it is usually formed through incremental policy analysis and the incremental "play of power." The ordinary citizen plays a passive role in policy determination, preferring to delegate policy-making power to a representative. But he can influence policy making through voting, political parties, and interest groups. The play of power occurs among the proximate makers of policy—the president, legislators, administrators, and judges. Lindblom notes the three characteristics of this play of power: (1) it is a process of formal and informal bargaining and cooperation among specialists, (2) policy analysis is subordinated to it, and (3) power is exerted according to rules.

Rehfuss, John. *Public Administration as Political Process.* New York, Charles Scribner's Sons, 1973. 248 pp.

Rehfuss views administrative behavior in public agencies as a political process. Concentrating on intergovernmental and agency politics, he argues that administrative practices and policies in government have a great impact on public attitudes toward the government and on public policy itself. Bureaucratic power is examined and related to the goals of federal agencies and the political environment of agency operations. State and local bureaucratic characteristics are surveyed and found to be similar to those of the federal bureaucracy, especially in political interactions.

Large-scale organizations, with their great size and insistence upon conformity, are seen as a threat to democracy and the individual. A review of traditional and contemporary organizational theory leads the author to conclude that no single theory is universally acceptable because of the complexity of large organizations. Chapters are devoted to a discussion of the characteristics of political and career bureaucratic executives; the policy-making process in public agencies including incrementalism and planning-programming-budgeting (PPB); comparative public administration; and past, present, and future values in public administration.

Rourke, Francis E. *Bureaucracy, Politics and Public Policy.* Boston, Little, Brown and Company, 1969. 174 pp.

An examination of the role played by agencies in the federal bureaucracy as primary participants in the policy-making process. The author lists the agency's sources of bureaucratic power as: (1) the cultivation of political support for agency policies in the general public, interest groups, and elected politicians and (2) bureaucratic expertise. Agencies vary greatly in their individual abilities to influence policy decisions. After examining the individual human participants in policy making within the federal agencies, the author discusses the effects exerted on the policy-making process by the bureaucratic environment. Three characteristics of this environment set it apart from the policy-making process of the legislature: hierarchy of authority, professionalism, and secrecy in policy deliberations. Dissatisfaction with policy making by bureaucrats has resulted in efforts to broaden the perspectives of bureaucrats, increase their use of quantitative methodology, and inspire more creativity and vigor. Rourke concludes with a discussion of the possible dangers for democracy as a result of this bureaucratic elite, sometimes alleged to control all government decision making without being subjected to any effective restrictions. He finds that, although the bureaucracy has a strong voice in public policy making, it is under constraints, the primary one being the competition of other elite groups.

Seidman, Harold. *Politics, Position, and Power: The Dynamics of Federal Organization.* New York, Oxford University Press, 1970. 312 pp.

An analysis of the American political system, focusing on the power structure in governmental departments, agencies, boards, institutes, foundations, and corporations. Writing from his experience as a former member of the staff of the United States Bureau of the Budget, Seidman believes that the real power rests with congressional leaders and private interests, calling federalism "cooperative feudalism." These multiple-power centers favor dilution of department heads' authority, thus causing great fragmentation in potentially cohesive social programs. He emphasizes the prevalence of professional or guild loyalties among those at all levels of government, administering programs or distributing funds. Seidman expresses the need for the president to centralize duties, to put aside dressings that make a program attractive and salable to Congress, and to concentrate on making the programs what they should be—effective for all elements in society. He concludes that Americans can no longer think of organization in terms of lines and boxes on an organizational chart. This is a well-written, comprehensive book for a general audience.

Steiner, Gilbert Y. *Social Insecurity: The Politics of Welfare*. Chicago, Rand McNally, 1966. 270 pp.

A well-documented study of the politics of public assistance in the United States. In developing his thesis that public assistance policy making is a failure, the author addresses himself to several problems and controversial issues in the area of welfare programs. He discusses the irrelevancy of the professional social worker's education and policy orientation, the unrealistic assumptions underlying the public's attitude toward welfare, the stagnancy of congressional welfare policy in view of a drastic change in the kinds and numbers of welfare clients, welfare cheating, and the politics of eligibility. Three major reasons for the poor state of affairs in the welfare policy-making process are identified: the automated nature of welfare policy making by Congress, the absence of presidential leadership, and the lack of meaningful interest-group participation. The author concludes by recommending enforced minimum standards for all categorical public assistance, replacement of old-age assistance as a welfare category with universal old-age insurance, and improved training for social workers.

Although this work has been somewhat dated by recent developments in the welfare field, such as increased demand for client participation and the resulting mobilization of welfare clients, it remains one of the few treatments of welfare politics available.

C. Intergovernmental Relations

Advisory Commission on Intergovernmental Relations. *Urban America and the Federal System.* Washington, D.C., U.S. Government Printing Office, 1969. 140 pp.

Policy recommendations on intergovernmental relations made in previous ACIR reports issued from 1961 to 1969 are summarized in this succinct volume. The major intergovernmental problems that have led to the urban crisis are reviewed. Emphasis is placed on the fiscal imbalance among federal, state, and local governments; the problems inherent in the continuing growth and development of urban areas; and outdated local government structures and authority relationships. The commission believes the state to be the weak link in the federal chain and recommends a course of action to strengthen it. The state's potential should be maximized so that it can properly perform its role as "keystone" of the federal system. Financial priorities of the states should place much more emphasis on urban affairs, and categorical grants-in-aid should be de-emphasized in favor of federal financial aid aimed at strengthening state and local governmental institutions. Diagrams and statistics are provided throughout. The appendix includes two case studies.

Other publications of ACIR are *Federalism in 1971: The Crisis Continues* (1972), *Profile of County Government: An Informational Report* (1972), *State Action on Local Problems* (1971), and *Fiscal Balance in the American Federal System* (2 vols., 1967). Single copies can be obtained without charge from the Advisory Commission on Intergovernmental Relations, Washington, D.C. 20575. Multiple copies of certain items can be purchased from the Superintendent of Documents, Government Printing Office, Washington, D.C. 20402.

Bollens, John C., in association with John R. Bayes and Kathryn L. Utter. *American County Government; with an Annotated Bibliography*. Beverly Hills, Calif., Sage Publications, 1969. 434 pp.

This book, the first major work on county government in America, reviews what is currently known about the 3,049 county governments and makes recommendations about the most productive areas for future study. The first part of the volume describes the general structural and functional characteristics of counties and lists research areas meriting exploration. An analytical framework for comparative study is then proposed, consisting of five political components: (1) resource utilization, (2) volume of intergovernmental linkages, (3) changes in organization and processes, (4) adequacy of public accountability, and (5) extent of voting competition in elections. The final section of the book is an extensive annotated bibliography of virtually everything written about county government, organized according to regions and functions.

Committee for Economic Development, Distribution Division, 477 Madison Ave., New York City, N.Y. 10022. Recent CED publications germane to the study of intergovernmental relations are *Modernizing Local Government* (1966, 84 pp.), recommending consolidation of fragmented local governments; *Fiscal Issues in the Future of Federalism* (1968, 88 pp.), assessing the fiscal problems of state and local governments and their future import; *Modernizing State Government* (1967, 86 pp.), which calls for the modernization of state constitutions; and *Reshaping Government in Metropolitan Areas* (1970, 84 pp.), urging a restructuring of metropolitan government toward a system that can deal more effectively with both metropolitan and community problems.

The CED publishes public and business policy statements in government, education, management, economics, and other areas. The books mentioned above and a list of other reasonably priced works can be obtained from the CED.

Derthick, Martha. *The Influence of Federal Grants: Public Assistance in Massachusetts.* Cambridge, Mass., Harvard University Press, 1970. 286 pp.

A study of the public assistance program in Massachusetts from 1936 to 1957. Its purpose is to analyze the federal grant-in-aid system as a means of influencing state and local governments to conform with national goals.

Federal influence on the Massachusetts public assistance programs is examined in terms of the development and administration of five national program goals: adequacy of assistance, equity of administration, efficiency of administration, provision of services, and professionalization of personnel.

The author finds that the federal government had a profound effect on modifying the state program, making it more uniform, centralized, and professionalized. However, state actions did not conform precisely to federal objectives because of limitations on the federal government's ability to enforce grant-in-aid conditions. The federal government's principal power was one of persuasion and diplomacy within a setting of continued negotiation.

Elazar, Daniel J. *American Federalism: A View from the States.* New York, Thomas Y. Crowell Company, 1966. 228 pp.

Elazar examines federalism from the traditional perspective of the states, which he sees as "political keystones, serving their local sub-divisions and supporting the overall structure of national government." His thesis is that the states are viable political institutions, each containing a civil society with its own individual political system and able to stand alone as a sovereign nation.

The author discusses three factors—political culture, sectionalism, and the continuing frontier—which determine the states' political structure, electoral behavior, and organization. He classifies the states according to three degrees of culture: individualistic, moralistic, and traditionalistic. Sectionalism results from natural groupings of states or parts of states which share common economic and social interests. The third factor, the continuing frontier, is the product of Americans' unceasing attempts to control the environment for their benefit and use.

Martin, Roscoe C. *The Cities and the Federal System.* New York, Atherton Press, 1965. 200 pp.

A book on the expanded federal partnership of national, state, and local governments, written from the viewpoint of the national and city partners. The author believes that the expansion of the federal-state relationship into a tripartite arrangement grew out of the states' ineffectiveness in coping with contemporary problems, such as increasing urbanization. It was made possible by the dynamic nature of the American federal system and its ability to adjust to new situations and demands.

After discussing the reasons for the states' ineffectiveness, the author traces the development of local government as a third partner in the federal system. He concludes with a look at federalism from the perspectives of Washington, D.C., the state capitol, and the community and an appraisal of the problems and consequences of the expanded federal system.

Reagan, Michael D. *The New Federalism.* New York, Oxford University Press, 1972. 176 pp.

Reagan believes that the old-style federalism, which emphasized a static, formal relationship between the states and the federal government, is dead. In its place a new federalism has evolved—a sharing concept incorporating dynamic responses to social, economic, and political factors. The author seeks to determine the best way to perform the principle function of the new federalism—the distribution of federal funds to the states.

Grants-in-aid have been the primary means of distributing funds and shaping intergovernmental relations, but revenue sharing has appeared as a substitute. Reagan describes and evaluates the concept of revenue sharing, presenting the case for and against its implementation. He concludes that revenue sharing is not the best method of allocating federal funds, primarily because of proved incapacities of state governments owing to such problems as structural inadequacies and corruption. The author's proposal: a "permissive federalism" in which state and national governments share power, with the state operating within broad policy areas established by Washington.

Sundquist, James L., with David W. Davis. *Making Federalism Work: A Study of Program Coordination at the Community Level.* Washington, D.C., Brookings Institution, 1969. 294 pp.

In offering a community perspective on federalism, the authors' major concerns are the problems and processes of program coordination at the local level.

Coordination problems were magnified in the 1960's as federal grants-in-aid became vehicles for fulfilling national rather than state and local goals. Although there was a massive increase in the flow of federal-grant dollars to state and local governments, this was accompanied by a corresponding decrease in the degree of program coordination.

The authors set out to determine what structures are needed, particularly at the community level, for better coordination. After studying the existing structures in urban poverty areas, concentrating on community-action agencies, model-cities programs, and various structures in underdeveloped rural areas, they conclude that two levels of co-operation are needed. For area coordination a broad and comprehensive multicounty organization is proposed; for coordination within a particular field, such as manpower or education, a single federal authority under the aegis of the executive office of the president is suggested. The authors conclude that, as community experience and expertise increase, federal and state government should increasingly defer to local judgment.

Wright, Deil S. *Federal Grants-in-Aid: Perspectives and Alternatives*. Washington, D.C., American Enterprise Institute, 1968. 158 pp.

This work discusses the federal grant-in-aid program and its alternatives and consequences and surveys previous studies of this method of distributing federal funds. After considering the legal basis and growth of the program, the author discusses grants-in-aid from the perspective of congressmen, who tend to divide along party lines in their points of view, and from the perspective of state and local officials and grant administrators, who show a great deal of ambivalence toward this form of aid. Wright sees two basic alternatives for improving the means of distributing federal aid to the states: modification of the grant-in-aid itself or the institution of a new mechanism to replace the grant. He considers the options available under each alternative, and decides that revenue sharing is the most efficacious substitution for the grant-in-aid.

D. Values, Technology, and Administration

Bronowski, J. *Science and Human Values*. 2d ed. New York, Harper and Row, Publishers, Inc., 1965. 120 pp.

Bronowski's classic work deals with the role of science in society. His theme is that the arts do not have a monopoly in contributing values to our culture. Science contributes just as much, if not more, and as a discipline of truth is the tie that binds society together.

Bronowski equates the scientist with the poet, writer, and painter, all of whom—in the discovery of a phenomenon of nature—perform creative acts. Scientists form a unique society, one in which justice, respect, and honor are key factors in teamwork. They cannot function unless they can work independently, are allowed to be original, and have the freedom to dissent. These are the values inherent in their profession, and these values comprise the legacy science leaves to mankind: the sense of human dignity.

Drucker, Peter F. *Technology, Management and Society*. New York, Harper and Row, Publishers, Inc., 1970. 210 pp.

A collection of twelve essays focusing on technology, management and its effect on the quality of life, and management within the enterprise. The author identifies management as a central social function and develops four main theses: (1) communication in organizations should originate with the intended recipients, (2) developments in society and the economy have forced changes in the fundamental assumptions underlying management as a discipline and as a practice, (3) in order to develop an adequate theory of business enterprise, one must understand the firm's survival objectives and the requirements for meeting these objectives, and (4) the purpose of management is not to be efficient but to be productive for the individual, the economy, and society. Drucker discusses such topics as management's new role, technological change, work and tools, the information explosion and communications gap, long-range planning, the use of computers, and management science.

Dvorin, Eugene P., and Robert H. Simmons. *From Amoral to Humane Bureaucracy*. San Francisco, Canfield Press, 1972. 88 pp.

Concerned with values in public administration and the governmental bureaucracy, the authors believe that administrators must avoid the dogmas of method and efficiency alone and "combine problem-solving with a sense of moral priorities." The need for this ensues from a "crisis of imbalance" in decision-making power that has left administrators in charge of the policy-making machinery of government. But administrators are not properly prepared to assume this leadership role because the teaching of public administration in the universities has resulted in too much emphasis on the vocational aspects of their profession, at the expense of theory. As a result public administrators lack the intellectual discipline needed to deal with a theory of values and to administer in accordance with moral responsibility. To develop moral responsibility, administrators must embrace "radical humanism," with man the primary concern of the bureaucracy and human dignity its ultimate end. An annotated bibliography is included.

Fuller, Richard Buckminster. *An Operating Manual for Spaceship Earth*. Carbondale, Southern Illinois University Press, 1969. 144 pp.

Fuller argues that science and technology are the best tools for resolving complex human and environmental problems. To maximize technology's ability to serve man, we must (1) eliminate the tunnel vision of narrowly educated specialists by stressing comprehensive knowledge and (2) clearly specify the operational goal of technology as making all humanity "comprehensively and sustainably successful." In his wide-ranging discussion Fuller defines wealth, tools, and technology and develops a metaphysical framework for moving man closer to a humane, scientific utopia.

Galbraith, John Kenneth. *Economics and the Public Purpose*. Boston, Houghton Mifflin Company, 1973. 334 pp.

Galbraith argues that the American economy consists of two parts, which he calls the "planning system" and the "market system." The planning system includes the giant, complex, technologically oriented firms, which, because of their size, dominate the economy and the government. The goal of the planning system is to maximize the growth of the firm and minimize uncertainties; neither competition nor supply and demand operate in the neoclassical economic sense. These organizations, partly because of their size and partly because of the expertise of the technostructure, exercise oligopolistic control over price, supply, demand, and the government. Aerospace, armaments, and pharmaceutical companies are examples of industries that extensively control their environment, hence the name "planning system."

The "market system," on the other hand, is the economy seen in operation on Main Street. The farmer, the repairman, the plumber, and the grocer are at the mercy of both supply and demand and the controlled prices and dominant political power of the planning system. Galbraith stresses that the unequal development of the power and wealth of the two systems results in dramatic deprivation where public need is greatest: in housing, health care, transportation, and environmental quality.

Galbraith proposes a series of economic, political, and social reforms for reducing the inequality between the two systems with a "new socialism" that is service-oriented rather than ideological.

Mosher, Frederick C. *Democracy and the Public Service.* New York, Oxford University Press, 1968. 220 pp.

This study examines the appointive public service in its relation to democratic ideals and practices. In particular, it addresses the question of how a protected public service, two or three times removed from direct participative democracy, can be made to operate in a manner compatible with democracy. Reliance upon elected representatives is one step removed from direct participative democracy. When representatives delegate powers to other officers appointed by them, a second step away from direct democracy is taken. A third step occurs when individuals are neither elected nor politically appointed but are chosen on the basis of certain criteria—such as social class, family, general competence, specialization in certain tasks and skills—and, once appointed, are shielded from removal on political grounds. In every developed country, most public employees belong in the last category. With the removal of public employees from direct electoral control as his primary concern, Mosher reviews the development of the American civil service— beginning with government by gentlemen during the Federalist era and ending with government by professionals—in terms of the values it has sought to represent. He deals with the ideological and philosophical background of the American public service, the various systems of public employment and the relations among them, education and the public service, the expanding role of the professions, and the unionization of public employees.

Mumford, Lewis. *The Myth of the Machine: The Pentagon of Power.* New York, Harcourt Brace Jovanovich, Inc., 1970. 496 pp.

Mumford takes a rather pessimistic approach in this wide-ranging discussion of human values and technology. Beginning his historical examination of man's relationship to the machine at the end of the fifteenth century—where a previous volume (*The Myth of the Machine: Technics and Human Development*) ended—he shows how technology has escaped from human control and gained primacy over man. The cause of this escape is man's relentless efforts to conquer nature through technology, while ignoring the need to control technology itself. The result is that our values reflect the ends and means of the technostructure: political absolutism, power, productivity, profit, and publicity. Mumford believes that man's attraction to technological progress for its own sake has been at the expense of his humanness and that it has led to such afflictions as alienation, neurosis, and loss of individual freedom.

Schmidt, Warren H. *Organizational Frontiers and Human Values*. Belmont, Calif., Wadsworth Publishing Company, Inc., 1970. 190 pp.

The author believes that man is living on a turbulent "frontier" of revolutionary change and crisis. His thesis is that man can better cope with this state of affairs if he can understand the values and assumptions being questioned in American society and learn how to keep his perspective through continuous learning experiences.

Great changes have occurred in life-styles, culture, and values, while organizations and institutions have remained essentially the same. This has resulted in much instability and uncertainty in the world and has led to such problems as the generation gap. To build a bridge across such chasms, the author recommends organizational development. Man must learn to manage his organizations during this period of change and crisis by developing the "leader-learner" style of manager who can continuously learn even while he leads.

Selected readings are included. Some of those particularly relevant to today's manager are "American Management: Everybody's Business," "Values, Man and Organizations," and "Primary Target for Change: The Manager or the Organization?" Futuristic publications become dated quickly, and this optimistic work is no exception. However, Schmidt presents an interesting view of anticipated social and cultural changes in the environment and their potential impact on organizations. An annotated bibliography is included.

Waldo, Dwight. *The Administrative State: A Study of the Political Theory of American Public Administration.* New York, Ronald Press, 1948. 228 pp.

A study of American public administration, outlining the discipline's underlying values and political premises. Waldo reviews the historical setting and social and ideological trends within the discipline and examines the philosophic orientations of its leading personalities. Five problems of political philosophy are employed in an analysis of the literature of public administration: the ends and ultimate values of the state; criteria for determining action; who should administer; the separation of powers; and centralization versus decentralization.

The author questions the validity of the "principles" of administration espoused by the scientific-management movement in business with underpinnings of economy and efficiency. He urges the development of a theory of administration based upon broader study and the recognition that public administration cannot be realistically or fruitfully studied apart from its political, social, or cultural setting.

Whisler, Thomas L. *Information Technology and Organizational Change.* Belmont, Calif., Wadsworth Publishing Company, Inc., 1970. 140 pp.

An overview of information technology and its influence on organizations and people, particularly managers, who must direct the adoption and use of computers in their organizations. Whisler believes that information technology produces anxiety and conflict among decision makers but that managers can diminish these problems by understanding the workings of complex organizations and technology, as well as the motivations of individuals.

The author traces the evolution of information technology and presents characteristics and problems of modern organizations. He discusses managerial duties—problem solving, communicating, goal setting—and views the manager as the link between organizations and the economy. While considering the impact of information technology on organizational structure, Whisler notes that the primary motivation for introducing computers into organizations is to increase managerial productivity. He cites the following effects of information technology on organizations: (1) a consolidation of activities and shrinkage of workers; (2) a reduction of levels of supervision and the number of people a supervisor must control; and (3) changes in departmentalization. The author concludes with a look at the future prospects and problems of information technology and includes a short history of the development of computer hardware.

Whyte, William H. *The Organization Man*. New York, Simon and Schuster, 1956. 430 pp.

A popular account of the growth of conformity in the white-collar echelons of big organizations. Whyte traces the origins of the ideology of the "organization man"—his education, ambitions, and anxieties—and the organizational and suburban environment that reinforces that ideology. He says that the individualism of the Protestant ethic has been replaced by a social ethic that worships the group. The major propositions of this social ethic are (1) that the group, not the individual, is the source of creativity, (2) that the ultimate individual need is to belong, and (3) that big organizations use the technology of social science to reinforce the ethic.

Whyte argues that the organization man is a new type, conforming willingly to the social ethic to gain a secure existence in an organization, thereby excluding himself as a source of creative and dynamic ideas for leadership and organizational growth.

146

VI. COMPARATIVE ADMINISTRATION

With the experiences of the Spaniards in Central and South America and the British in India, the problems of administration in different cultures had become known by the eighteenth century. The colonization of Africa in the nineteenth century further illuminated the complexity of administration in foreign territories. This complexity has still not been fully understood by some administrators.

Significant American involvement with administration in foreign countries can be traced to Herbert Hoover and his efforts as head of the Relief Administration in Europe following World War I.

When the military victories of World War II secured foreign territory, the American government provided "foreign aid" to help the war-ravaged and the newly independent nations, and United States companies quickly began to move into these new market areas.

Administrators involved in efforts to assist technically and to modernize public management in different cultures soon realized the need for studying the effects of cultural environment on public administration. Questions arose about which elements of administration were transferable. Some realized that, for administration to be a science, its canons had to possess universality. It became readily apparent that occidental bureaucratic theory—with its peculiar cultural and religious underpinnings operating within a highly differentiated industrial society—was inadequate for the study of bureaucracies operating within functionally diffuse, agrarian societies.

By studying cross-cultural administration, the public administrator in the United States (for example, the Department of the Interior) could better grasp the pitfalls of culturally insensitive administration. Increasingly the international American corporation must be cognizant of the public administrative environment in other countries or once again will find it necessary to call upon the American government to intervene.

The books in this section provide the administrator—public and private—with some understanding of the cultural limitations of our administrative tools, concepts, and proverbs in different administrative settings. The books point out that we can learn as much from the workings of other nations' administrative systems as we can contribute and that, while the implementation of program-planning-budgeting has been stymied in the United States, it has enjoyed steady progress and successful utilization in many other countries.

Boddewyn, J., *et al. World Business Systems and Environments.* Scranton, Pa., International Textbook Company, 1972. 514 pp.

This book explores business systems and their environmental settings in five regions: Asia, Latin America, the Middle East, Sub-Saharan Africa, and Western Europe. The economic, political, social, and cultural environment of each region is examined and related to the state of enterprise development, patterns of management, financial markets and practices, marketing institutions and methods, and the role and state of industrial relations. The homogeneity and heterogeneity present in the environments and business systems in each region are identified. While the historical development of each region is briefly reviewed, the emphasis of the book is on current business practices.

Dalby, Michael T., and Michael S. Werthman, eds. *Bureaucracy in Historical Perspective*. Glenview, Ill., Scott, Foresman and Company, 1971. 178 pp.

This book of readings examines bureaucracy from an international and historical perspective. Each selection concerns an important aspect of the governmental bureaucratic organization under one of the following topics: the role of bureaucracy in society, problems of personnel, bureaucratic behavior, control of bureaucracy, and the impact of bureaucracy on society. Articles treat the governmental bureaucracies of Britain, Imperial China, the Ottoman Empire, Spain, Prussia, Russia, the United States, and New York City. The works of sociologists, historians, and practicing administrators are included. Among the authors: Max Weber, E. N. Gladden, S. N. Eisenstadt, and Hyman G. Rickover.

Farmer, Richard N. and Barry M. Richman. *Comparative Management and Economic Progress*. Bloomington, Ind., Cedarwood Publishing Company, 1970. 436 pp.

Farmer and Richman maintain that the variables in political, economic, cultural, and educational environments have a direct and significant impact on managerial and industrial effectiveness. The domestic manager has acquired a familiarity with the domestic environment that he consciously or subconsciously employs in making decisions. Many of the problems of the foreign administrator result from the strangeness of the environment in which he must operate, and his success depends in part on his ability to assess and adjust properly to that environment. The authors thus stress environmental analysis as the foundation of an understanding of international management. Key environmental variables are identified and discussed, and their relationship to the functions of management is explored. Using many illustrations, the authors demonstrate how different patterns of management around the world result from differences in environment.

Heady, Ferrel. *Public Administration: A Comparative Perspective*. Englewood Cliffs, N.J., Prentice-Hall, Inc., 1966. 116 pp.

An introduction to comparative public administration that focuses on the public bureaucracy of various nations as the basis for comparison. Although the author finds no standard pattern of relationships between the bureaucracy and the political system as a whole, he concludes that there are factors that have an important effect on these relationships, including the political development of the country, the characteristics of a political regime, and the nature of bureaucratic goals.

After a survey of the state of the art of comparative administration, Heady explores structural and behavioral variations among public bureaucracies. He traces the political and administrative evolution of the developed nations, briefly describing administration in France, Germany, Britain, the United States, Japan, and the Soviet Union. Characteristics of administration in less developed countries are also examined, including the ideology and politics of development and common administrative patterns. Special emphasis is placed on relationships between bureaucracies and the political systems in which they operate.

Novick, David. *Current Practice in Program Budgeting (PPBS) Analysis and Case Studies Covering Government and Business.* New York, Crane, Russak and Company, Inc., 1973. 242 pp.

This work documents the development of PPBS in the United States and abroad to the end of 1971. The author devotes early chapters of the book to the setting of PPBS and an analysis of the concept itself—what it is and what it is not. Novick notes that, although PPBS originated in the United States, it has virtually perished as far as Washington, D.C., is concerned. It has gained strength abroad, however, where the approach to PPBS has been more cautious and pragmatic, with greater concern for the process as a whole and the difficulties in its implementation.

The rest of the volume consists of twenty-one case histories of PPBS in nine countries, two state governments in the United States, several local governments in the United States and abroad, two business firms, and various other organizations.

Raphaeli, Nimrod, ed. *Readings in Comparative Public Administration.* Boston, Allyn and Bacon, 1967. 490 pp.

This book is devoted to three subjects: (1) individual bureaucratic systems in various cultures, (2) development administration, and (3) conceptual, analytical, and ecological aspects of comparative public administration. The bureaucratic systems examined include those of China, France, Britain, and the Soviet Union. The section on development administration provides a general treatment of the institution of bureaucracy in less developed countries. The final section includes theoretical positions from such leading scholars in the field as Wallace Sayre, S. N. Eisenstadt, Ferrel Heady, and Fred Riggs. The editor includes an overview of comparative public administration that traces the field through its roots, stages of development, and major trends and emphases. A lengthy bibliography is included.

Riggs, Fred W. *Administration in Developing Countries: The Theory of Prismatic Society*. Boston, Houghton Mifflin Company, 1964. 477 pp.

Riggs takes a pan-disciplinary approach to the study of administration in developing nations by building a "prismatic model" of transitional society. A prismatic society exists along a theoretical continuum, stretching from the polar opposites of fused, or traditional, society, and diffracted, or modern, society, combining various elements of both. The prismatic model encompasses the ecology of administration in transitional societies, considering administrative structures and functions in the broad context of their social, economic, political, and cultural environment.

The paradoxical nature of public administration in a prismatic society is explained by the author's "sala model" of bureaucratic behavior. Elements of sala public administration include "bazaar canteen" economic features, nepotism in bureaucratic recruitment, institutionalized corruption, a bureaucratic emphasis on personal power and gain at the public expense, inefficiency in the application of rules, and a large gap between prescribed behavior and actual behavior (formalism). Riggs uses the sala model to deal with such matters as the weight and scope of bureaucratic power, administrative obstacles to economic development, public finance, personnel administration, communications, and local-government administration.

Rowat, Donald C. *The Ombudsman Plan: Essays on the Worldwide Spread of an Idea*. Toronto, McClelland and Stewart, 1973. 330 pp.

A handbook on the ombudsman institution as it exists throughout the world. The essays emphasize the flexibility of the office, which has facilitated its adaptation to diverse systems of government.

After discussing the ombudsman's origin in the Scandinavian countries, Rowat explains the need for the institution in other countries and illustrates its historical development and application in North America. The text of the book concludes with a look at the worldwide spread of the idea of the ombudsman.

A lengthy appendix contains reviews of other publications concerning the ombudsman, a bibliography of recent materials, and new ombudsman laws and proposals from various nations, including Australia, Canada, the United States, and Israel.

APPENDICES

APPENDIX I. SELECTED JOURNALS

Academy of Management Journal (quarterly). Graduate School of Business, Indiana University, Bloomington, Indiana 47401.

Administration in Mental Health. U.S. Department of Health, Education, and Welfare, Superintendent of Documents, U.S. Government Printing Office, Washington, D.C. 20000.

Administrative Science Quarterly. Graduate School of Business and Public Administration, Cornell University, Ithaca, N.Y. 14850.

Advanced Management Journal (quarterly). Society for the Advancement of Management, 16 W. 40th St., New York City, N.Y. 10018.

American County Government (monthly). National Association of Counties, 101 Connecticut Ave., N.W., Washington, D.C. 20036.

Business Quarterly. School of Business Administration, University of Western Ontario, London, Canada.

The Bureaucrat (quarterly). National Capital Area Chapter of the American Society for Public Administration, NCSL Publications, 1825 K St., N.W., Washington, D.C. 20006.

California Management Review (quarterly). Graduate School of Business Administration, University of California, Berkeley, Calif. 94720.

Canadian Public Administration (quarterly). Institute of Public Administration of Canada, 897 Bay St., Toronto 5, Ontario, Canada.

Comparative Local Government (biannual). International Union of Local Authorities, 45 Wassenaarseweg, The Hague, Netherlands.

Educational Administration Quarterly. University Council for Educational Administration, 29 W. Woodruff Ave., Columbus, Ohio 43210.

Evaluation: A Forum for Human Service Decision-Makers. Program Evaluation Project, 501 S. Park Ave., Minneapolis, Minn. 55415.

Good Government (quarterly). National Civil Service League, 1825 K Street, N.W., Washington, D.C. 20006.

Harvard Business Review (bimonthly). Graduate School of Business Administration, Harvard University, Soldiers Field, Boston, Mass. 02163.

Hospital Administration (quarterly). American College of Hospital Administrators, 840 N. Lake Shore Dr., Chicago, Ill. 60611.

Hospital Management (monthly). Hospital Management, Inc., 105 W. Adams St., Chicago, Ill.   60600.

Indian Journal of Public Administration (quarterly). Indian Institute of Public Administration, Indraprastha Estate, Ring Road (East), New Delhi-110001, India.

International Review of Administrative Sciences (quarterly). International Institute of Administrative Sciences, Rue de la Charite 15, B-1040, Brussels, Belgium.

Management Research (monthly). P.O. Box 4, Dolton, Ill. 60419.

Management Review (monthly). American Management Association, 135 W. 50th St., New York, N.Y.   10020.

Midwest Review of Public Administration (quarterly). Park College, Parkville, Mo.   64152.

Nation's Cities (monthly). National League of Cities, 1612 K Street, N.W., Washington, D.C.   20006.

Personnel Administration (bimonthly). Society for Personnel Administration, 1221 Connecticut Ave., N.W., Washington, D.C.   20036.

Personnel Bibliography Series. U.S. Civil Service Commission, Washington, D.C.   20415.

Philippine Journal of Public Administration (quarterly). P.O. Box 474, Manila, Philippines.

Psychology Today (monthly). Box 2990, Boulder, Colo. 20302.

Public Administration (quarterly). Royal Institute of Public Administration, 24 Park Crescent, London W.I., England.

Public Administration Review (quarterly). American Society for Public Administration, 1329 18th St., N.W., Washington, D.C.   20036.

Public Management (monthly). International City Managers Association, 1140 Connecticut Ave., N.W., Washington, D.C.   20036.

Public Personnel Review (quarterly). Public Personnel Association, 1313 E. 60th St., Chicago, Ill.   60637.

Society (bimonthly). Box A, Rutgers—the State University, New Brunswick, N.J.   08903.

State Government (quarterly). Council of State Governments, 1313 E. 60th St., Chicago, Ill.   60637.

Training and Development Journal (monthly). American Society for Training and Development, Inc., 313 Price Pl., P.O. Box 5307, Madison, Wis.   53705.

APPENDIX II. SELECTED REFERENCES

ANBAR Publications provides selected abstracts from more than 200 journals, including foreign-language sources. The abstracts are published eight times a year in five journals: *Top Management Abstracts, Personnel and Training, Accounting and Data Processing, Marketing and Distribution, Work Study and Organization and Management.* Specimen copies are available on request from ANBAR Publications, P.O. Box 23, Wembley   HA9   8DJ, England.

The Bi-Monthly Review of Management Research, a research reference journal, lists and abstracts new books and journal articles in such areas of business management as general administration, human resources, labor relations, and career training. Available from Management Research, P.O. Box 4, Dolton, Ill.   60419.

Communication in Organizations—A Guide to Information Sources. Robert M. Carter. Detroit, Gale Research Company, 1972. 272 pp.

An annotated bibliography and sourcebook on organizational communication. The subjects include theories and systems of organizational communication, barriers, oral and written channels of communication, organizational change including kinds of training to effect change, and evaluation studies of the effectiveness of organizational communication. A section is devoted to general works, and a list of addresses of periodical and book publishers is given. Comprehensive guides to the contents are provided in name, title, and subject indexes.

The Encyclopedia of Management. 2d ed. Edited by Carl Heyel. New York, Van Nostrand Reinhold Company, 1973. 1161 pp.

Virtually every subject with which modern managers deal is given in-depth treatment in this work. The contributions of well-known practitioners and scholars are arranged alphabetically by subject matter from "Accounting" to "Zero Defects." The editor asserts that the reader can acquire an understanding of the fundamental concerns of management, enabling him to ask the right kinds of questions of specialists and technicians both within and outside his organization.

Handbook of Business Administration. Edited by Harold Bright Maynard. New York, McGraw-Hill Book Company, 1967.

This massive work, containing 166 chapters grouped into 17 sections, is designed to serve the needs of practicing managers and those who aspire to become better managers. In addition to the initial 31 chapters, which relate to organization, general management, and the common concerns of all managers, the sections most relevant to managers of vocational rehabilitation organizations are: "Accounting and Control," "Management of Human Resources," "Managing External Relations," "Office Administration," "Systems and Data Processing," and "Tools and Techniques of Management Decision-Making and Control."

Handbook of Modern Office Management and Administrative Services. Edited by Carl Heyel. New York, McGraw-Hill Book Company, 1972. 1172 pp.

A reference work on office management, providing practical information for effective organization and management in the business or government office. Information is provided on the environment of the office, including space planning, furnishing, maintenance, and security, and on the functions of personnel administration, such as interviewing, testing, paying, and evaluating the employee. One section is devoted to the organization and management of administrative services, such as printing, copying, stenography, filing, and correspondence. Other areas covered by the book are managing and improving office operations, training for office operations, office personnel relations, achieving supervisory effectiveness, and data processing.

Handbook of Modern Personnel Administration. Edited by Joseph J. Famular. New York, McGraw-Hill Book Company, 1972. 1268 pp.

This handbook is designed to provide authoritative information on all aspects of modern personnel administration. It employs a practical approach to personnel problems for personnel administrators, supervisors, and students and attempts to provide solutions to most of the personnel problems one is likely to encounter on the job. Some section titles: "Organization and Operation of the Personnel Administration Department," "Wage and Salary Administration,"

"Employee Appraisal and Assessment," "International Personnel Management," "Special Personnel Problems," and "Communicating to Employees." The handbook also contains information on testing and interviewing of applicants; the orientation of new employees; evaluation of office, plant, technical, supervisory, and sales personnel; establishment of a wage and salary program; equal employment; employee termination; and the writing of an employee handbook.

Handbook of Organizations. Edited by James G. March. Chicago, Rand McNally, 1965. 1248 pp.

The editor of this scholarly book identified his "simple" objective as an attempt "to summarize and report the present state of knowledge about human organizations." One evidence of how well the thirty-two contributors have succeeded may be the twenty-five page index of authors. It does not purport to be a how-to book, and it is not; however, it is readable and (except for a few chapters on specific institutions) relevant to the managerial tasks in vocational-rehabilitation agencies. The editor concludes his introduction in the following manner: "We think the study of organizations and human behavior within organizations is important. We also think it is fun."

Lesly's Public Relations Handbook. 4th ed. Edited by Philip Lesly. Englewood Cliffs, N.J., Prentice-Hall, Inc., 1971. 558 pp.

The latest edition of this pioneering handbook, first published in 1950, consists of contributions from forty-one public relations practitioners. The scope of public relations, organizational uses of public relations, the technique of communication, and trends in public relations are some of the major subjects. The book provides a good overview of the field, setting forth proved techniques and step-by-step instructions for planning, initiating, and maintaining a public relations program.

The National Civil Service League and its service project, the National Program Center for Public Personnel Management, offer a wide variety of publications, including four annual issues of *Advance: Studies in Public Manpower Modernization*, the quarterly magazine *Good Government*, and to twelve annual issues of *NCSL Exchange*, a manpower newsletter. Examples of other publications offered for sale: *Pacemaker: A Handbook for Civil Service Change, Revenue Sharing and Manpower Programs, The Disadvantaged and Government Jobs,* and *Training and Testing of the Disadvantaged.* Information about the organization and its publications may be obtained from National Civil Service League, 1825 K St., N.W., Washington, D.C.   20006.

Organization Development: An Annotated Bibliography. Edited by Jerome L. Franklin. Center for Research on Utilization of Scientific Knowledge, Institute for Social Research. Ann Arbor, University of Michigan, 1973.

This annotated bibliography of organization development includes material from books and journals, and covers a wide range of topics: theory, case studies, empirical investigations, conceptual models, and commonly used techniques of OD. The abstracts summarize major ideas and topics in the books and articles. A list of contributors is included. Materials are arranged alphabetically by author. An author index and an index of topics follow the abstracts.

Training and Development Handbook. Edited by Robert L. Craig and Lester R. Bittel. New York, McGraw-Hill Book Company, 1967. 650 pp.

Sponsored by the American Society for Training and Development, this work was edited by the editors of the *Training and Development Journal* and *Factory Magazine*. The thirty-six contributors are, in the main, responsible for training and development of human resources in the organizations with which they are affiliated. Emphasis is given to training methods and the managerial aspects of planning, organizing, assembling resources, and controlling and evaluating a training program. Technical terminology is avoided. Most chapters include references and bibliography.

INDEX OF AUTHORS

Index of Authors

INDEX OF TITLES

Index of Titles